BUILD

STUFF WITH

WOOD

Make Awesome Projects with Basic Tools

BUILD

STUFF WITH

WOOD

Make Awesome Projects with Basic Tools

The Taunton Press

The Taunton Press, Inc.

63 South Main Street

Newtown, CT 06470-2344

Email: tp@taunton.com

Editor: Peter Chapman

Copy Editor: Seth Reichgott

Jacket/Cover Design: Stacy Wakefield Forte

Interior Design and Layout: Stacy Wakefield Forte

Photographer: Asa Christiana except as follows: p. 2 Mark Lohman; p. 8 (bottom) and p. 9 (bottom right) Steve Scott, courtesy of *Fine Woodworking*; p. 9 (top right) courtesy of Mark Edmundson; p. 9 (center left) courtesy of Jimmy Diresta; p. 15 (top center and top right) Andy Engel, courtesy of *Fine Homebuilding*; p. 25 (top right) David Heim, courtesy of *Fine Woodworking*; p. 80 ©Duane Bolland; p. 111 (top right) ©John Sterling; p. 111 (center left) Tom Begnal, courtesy of *Fine Woodworking*; p. 111 (bottom right) ©Chris Guibert

Illustrator: Dan Thornton

The following names/manufacturers appearing in *Build Stuff with Wood* are trademarks: Atari®, Battleship®, Bluetooth®, DeWalt®, eBay®, Erector®, Forest Stewardship Council®, FSC®, Habitat for Humanity®, I-Semble®, IKEA®, Lee Valley®, Lego®, Lie-Nielsen®, Lincoln Logs®, Minwax®, Monopoly®, My Little Pony®, Operation®, Rockler®, Starr®, Super Glue®, Tinkertoy®, Titebond III®, Trouble®, Velcro®, Veritas®, Woodcraft®, X-Acto®

Library of Congress Cataloging-in-Publication Data

    Names: Christiana, Asa, author.

  Title: Build stuff with wood : make awesome projects with basic tools / Asa Christiana.

  Description: Newtown, CT : Taunton Press, Inc., [2017]

  Identifiers: LCCN 2017007163 | ISBN 9781631867118

  Subjects: LCSH: Woodwork.

  Classification: LCC TT180 .C455 2017 | DDC 684/.08--dc23

  LC record available at https://lccn.loc.gov/2017007163

About Your Safety: Working wood is inherently dangerous. Using hand or power tools improperly or ignoring safety practices can lead to permanent injury or even death. Don't try to perform operations you learn about here (or elsewhere) unless you're certain they are safe for you. If something about an operation doesn't feel right, don't do it. Look for another way. We want you to enjoy the craft, so please keep safety foremost in your mind whenever you're in the shop.

dedication

To Grandpa Sam, who
was steadfast and kind

ACKNOWLEDGMENTS

I FEEL LIKE I've been preparing most of my life to write this book, so I have a lot of people to thank.

As a freshman in tech school, I met Mr. Brooks, the lead instructor in the machine tool program, a brilliant guy who was born to work with kids like me. He nurtured my spark and set me on a path of lifelong creativity.

I was just as lucky at my first newspaper job, where I found the mentor every young writer needs. My boss on the Living Section was Ken Heidel, who taught me how to cut the fat and trust my talent.

When I arrived at *Fine Woodworking* magazine, Chief Editor Tim Schreiner showed me how a good magazine gets made and Senior Editor Anatole Burkin hung in there patiently through my daily barrage of questions. Later, as my boss, Anatole tried his best to teach me that less is more (I never quite accepted that!) and how a leader is different from a do-er (another tough lesson). On behalf of myself and a small army of other idealistic, creative people, I owe a great debt to The Taunton Press, which has given its editors and art directors the resources to make unmatched how-to content and empower four decades of makers.

I had more mentors at Taunton than I can list, but it would be a crime not to thank the multi-talented Mike Pekovich, *Fine Woodworking*'s long-serving art director and my main collaborator for more than a decade. Mike taught me how to be a better woodworker and a passable photographer, but most important, he quietly helped me steer the ship for eight years, matching my passion for the mission at every turn.

For helping me to exit the job gracefully and prepare for my next adventure as a freelancer, I have to thank Anatole Burkin once again. Speaking of graceful, no one is more thoughtful and steady at the wheel than my worthy successor, Tom McKenna.

It was a lucky day when I was asked to appear on *The Martha Stewart Show* in 2011. The guest of honor that day was Nick Offerman, who played Ron Swanson on the NBC comedy *Parks and Recreation*. Turns out he was a *Fine Woodworking* super-fan. Once I learned just how skilled he was in his own woodshop, one of his clever jigs soon ended up in the magazine and his bearded face appeared on the cover. Nick repaid us by bringing the magazine on all of his celebrity rounds, from late night talk shows to podcasts to Reddit. His excellent foreword to this book is just another gift from the most generous person I know.

That brings us to the present, and to my biggest debt of all. I owe everything to my wife, Lynne. For making this crazy move with me and our girls to Portland, Oregon. For never blinking when I said I wanted to trade a secure job at *Fine Woodworking* for the unpredictable life of a freelance writer, furniture maker, and lord knows what else. For dropping her career and picking up another to make sure we could pay the bills when we rolled into town with two cars, one daughter, and a dog. Without her encouragement and support, I would not have been able to get this book out of my head and into the world.

TABLE OF CONTENTS

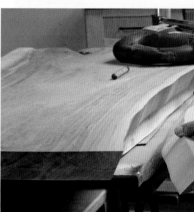

foreword

I HAVE ALWAYS BEEN DRAWN to people who make things with their hands. This attraction has afforded me the opportunity to shake some of the most creative mitts I could chase down, in the hope that some of their derring-do would rub off on my own paws. That is how I came to meet Asa Christiana in 2011 on the set of Martha Stewart's television program. At the time he was the editor of my woodworking bible, *Fine Woodworking* magazine, which meant he was the central brain behind all of the master craftspersons from whom I gleaned my sawdusty tutelage. In superhero terms, he was Professor Xavier to the X-Men (and women) in the pages of *FWW,* and so I was as giddy as a dancing faun to make his acquaintance.

Over the years of our friendship, I have shamelessly exploited his generosity with his vast knowledge in the realms of tools and wood species and machinery and people to my own advantage, as his mind is a vault of information that could be called upon to establish a woodworking school, or write a terribly rarefied book about building intricate pieces of museum-quality furniture. The hitch with such a book, however nifty the artistry therein, is that, in its specialization, it would alienate the vast majority of curious readers. Thankfully, by here offering an instructional book that relies more upon the reader's gumption than his or her collection of fancy chisels, Asa has taken a mighty swing in the other direction.

In this age of rampant consumerism, a great many of our citizens have come to enjoy the luxuries afforded us by purchasable goods. This trend has had a softening effect that has seen a large percentage of our population grow befuddled when it comes to the knowledge of the hammer or the Phillips-head screwdriver. If

> **With Asa's clear and affable writing, a simple set of tools, and the affordable materials available at any home improvement store, the world is indeed your oyster.**

you are looking for a route that navigates a return to such knowledge, by which you can get started making furniture and accessories for your home, but you do not have years of shop experience under your belt, then look no further. You are holding the finest of roadmaps in your hands even now.

When I was a bachelor in my twenties, I became obsessed with building furniture for my apartment out of lumber that I found in alleys or construction dumpsters. Armed with a jigsaw and a screw gun, I built a variety of pieces from bookshelves to tables to a simple desk in much the same way the projects in this book are assembled—relying more upon ingenuity and thrift than expensive machinery. Although my furnishings never won any awards, they made me feel incredibly proud of my self-sufficiency, and their groovy, handmade style did excite a great deal of commentary from my guests. While I am a student of a more rarefied brand of woodworking these days, I recognize and applaud the power that Asa's lessons will unleash in your life. Many of our modern homes and budgets may not be conducive to the accretion of tablesaws and pickup trucks, but that doesn't mean that you can't enjoy a life bolstered by making swell furniture and home accessories.

My favorite aspect of this book is the flat-out fun that courses through the creation of every project. Asa suggests some really hip furniture designs, but it's also readily apparent that you can alter his plans to meet your own desires. His coffee table, to name one example, illustrates the malleability of these projects, since the author himself could not decide between two designs and so he built them both. What then, with this in mind, is to keep you from altering any of the designs within to fit your own fancy? With Asa's clear and affable writing, a simple set of tools, and the affordable materials available at any home improvement store, the world is indeed your oyster. Have fun!

— Nick Offerman

introduction: why we build

ANALOG FUN. When I was a kid, we made big frontier forts with Lincoln Logs. Legos were a huge hit too.

LOOKING BACK on my childhood in the 1970s—days of collecting old lumber and nails to make "forts" in the woods and fixing up my beater bikes with parts cannibalized from other beater bikes—I remember the day the world changed.

Before that day, we built stuff for fun. With only four channels of TV, kids my age filled their time with Tinkertoys®, Lincoln Logs®, and Legos® (and comic books). Once you were old enough to be left alone with an X-Acto® knife and solvent glue, you were ready to build models: model cars, model planes, and model rockets.

I loved the rockets most. If you grew up post-1980, you probably don't know how cool it is to build your own rocket from a cardboard tube and wood fins, load a black-powder "engine" in it, pack in the parachute, stick on the nose cone, slide the rocket onto its guide wire, and turn the switch on a battery pack to ignite the engine and shoot your creation 1,000 ft. into the blue sky—hoping for a tiny pop of color that meant the parachute had worked (phew!) and you could run through the neighborhood tracking your investment on the summer wind.

Like model rockets and model trains, our games were analog, too: Battleship®, Operation®, Monopoly®, Trouble®. But one game changed everything.

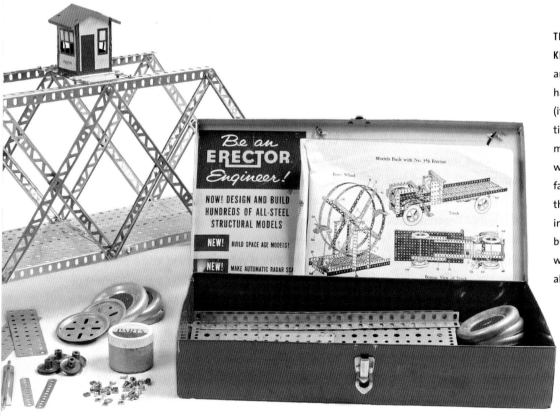

THE ULTIMATE MAKER KIT. In the 1950s and 1960s, kids had "Erector®" sets (it was a simpler time—there were men named Dick), with little steel struts, fasteners, and pulleys that could be turned into everything from bridges to trucks to working machines of all kinds.

BACK TO
THE WOODS

Wood lets you build all sorts
of stuff in the real world.

FROM FUN TO FINE.
I had just as much
fun building painted
furniture for my kids
as I did this fine oak
Morris chair.

YOUR IMAGINATION IS THE LIMIT. A woodworking friend, Mark Edmundson, who lives in a remote spot in northern Idaho, built this huge skate park for his kids, section by section. He had never done it before, so he just dove in and learned as he went. That's the best approach.

USE THIS BOOK AS A SPRINGBOARD. With a few basic techniques under your belt, you'll be ready to take on all sorts of wood crafts, from building a guitar to building a cedar-strip canoe, like this one by another woodworking buddy, Nick Offerman (of NBC's *Parks and Recreation*).

start with wood and then break the rules

In my book (literal and figurative), the best medium for building things is wood, and so wood is our weapon of choice here. It has a strength-to-weight ratio that rivals titanium and carbon fiber, yet you can cut and shape and join it with simple tools. Better yet, wood has soul. It is a renewable, organic material that comes in hundreds of species, each with its own special luster, each board with its own swirling grain patterns—making every wood project unique.

Wood also comes in many forms, from reclaimed, rough-milled, and smooth-planed to wood composites like plywood and MDF. And all of them are widely available.

> If you throw out the old woodworking rules, you can add whatever you want to your pile of boards and plywood.

But wood isn't the whole story here. If you throw out the old woodworking rules, you can add whatever you want to your pile of boards and plywood. Home centers are full of nuts, bolts, pipes, brackets, screws, and all sorts of cool hardware you can use to build things. Go online—for weird lights, magnets, wheels, bottle openers, and a thousand other oddities—and the fun multiplies.

So this isn't your granddad's woodworking book. Don't let anyone tell you there are rules, because there aren't, other than staying safe. That said, if you dream of fine woodworking, carpentry, remodeling, boat-building, instrument-making, or any other traditional woodcraft, this book will serve as a great introduction to the fundamental tools and skills you'll need to get started.

start where you are

With just a small amount of space and a few tools, you can build everything in this book. And though these projects are easy and fun, they won't make you look like a beginner. Why take the time to build something that isn't useful, durable, and awesome-looking? I wrote this book to show you how easy it is to make something great.

By sticking with widely available lumber that is ready to use off the shelf, you can avoid the big machines required for smoothing and milling boards to special sizes. Another trick is using bolts and screws to hold things together, letting you avoid complicated wood joints, at least for now.

None of these decisions are compromises. By breaking the rules, you'll make woodworking more fun, while making projects that are just as cool as the traditional stuff, maybe cooler.

build projects, build skills, and collect a few tools

I have arranged these projects as a progression, so you build your skills and your tool collection as you go. You don't have to follow that plan, but be warned: If you jump around, you'll find that later projects skip over techniques described earlier in the book.

In the next chapter, you'll learn how to set up a simple workspace, how to choose your first tools, and where to find the wood and other supplies you'll need. One of the first projects is a mobile workstation, built from a surplus kitchen cabinet that you can buy almost anywhere. You can build every project in this book on that rolling cabinet—though it wouldn't hurt to have another work surface, like a sturdy table.

Although I provide drawings and dimensions for each project, don't hesitate to put those aside and make whatever you want with the tools, techniques, and ideas you find in this book.

Let's get started then. That's the secret, by the way: Just diving in. Remember that.

WHY WOOD?

EASY TO CUT AND SHAPE. You can work wood with relatively simple tools.

EVERY BOARD IS DIFFERENT. Wood is an organic, renewable material that offers an endless array of colors and grain patterns. By the way, this is white oak, which can have crazy tiger stripes in it.

PLEASURE VS. SATISFACTION. The satisfaction of building something real runs deeper than forwarding a puppy video or binge-watching *The Bachelor*.

gearing up: where to build and what to build with

I WROTE THIS book for everyone, especially people with no skills, no tools (yet), and very limited space. You can carve out a small workspace almost anywhere—in a spare room or in the corner of your garage or basement.

The only hitch might be the noise from power tools. If your neighbors are on the other side of a wall, floor, or ceiling, you might have to work while they are out, or maybe find a book on woodworking with hand tools only. There are lots of good ones out there.

Speaking of hand tools, I think the fastest way to learn how to build things—and the easiest way to get things done—is with power tools, at least at first. I love the precision of handplanes and chisels, but they require a fair amount of sharpening gear and experience to get them to work well. I've seen a lot of newbies commit themselves to the romance of old-timey tools only to get paralyzed along the learning curve. This book is about getting things built, and having fun doing it.

WHERE TO BUILD

It all starts with setting up shop, which is nothing more than creating some space and storage and buying a few key tools.

You can build all of the projects in this book in a very small area. You'll need at least one sturdy table or workbench, but two will be better. One of your main tools will be a miter saw, which is a benchtop power tool, and it's nice to be able to keep it on a table ready to go.

The other table is for building and assembling projects. Whether you are drilling holes, cutting plywood, driving screws, or whatever, it's usually most comfortable to work at waist height.

On the walls, I'm not a huge fan of pegboard or cabinets. I find simple shelves to be a lot more convenient. If there is drywall on the walls, be sure to find the studs and screw into those when attaching shelves.

BRIGHTEN YOUR CORNER. You can build projects in an 8-ft. by 10-ft. space or less. White walls and a window will brighten up the place. Add some shelving and a couple of worktables and you're ready to roll. In the next chapter, we'll use a surplus kitchen cabinet to build the rolling workstation you see below the window.

In a basement, you'll need to first attach some 2×4s flat to the concrete wall using powder-actuated nails (available at any home center), and then attach the shelves to those.

Wood shelves are great because you can stack lumber and supplies on them, drill and saw through them to create tool holders, and store your clamps on them, too, by simply clamping them on.

By the way, it's nice to have a window or two for natural light and the occasional view of the wide world. We moved out of caves for a reason. Also, a can of white paint goes a long way. White walls reflect light and will make your garage or basement much brighter without buying a single bulb.

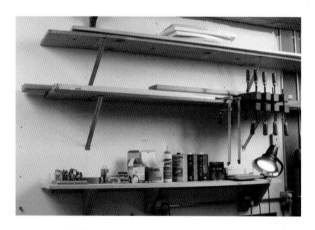

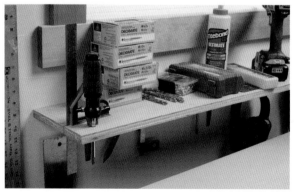

WOOD SHELVES ADD SIMPLE, EFFECTIVE STORAGE. Shelf brackets are cheap and strong, and any boards will do. You can drill and saw shelves to create tool holders (above), pile boards and supplies on them, and attach clamps to them for storage (top).

let there be light

I learned long ago that if you aren't comfortable and can't see well in your workspace, you won't have as much fun there. You might even start to avoid it. On the other hand, if your shop area is well-lit and at least 55 degrees, you won't hesitate to throw on a hoodie (or a snappy sweater vest) and spend time there. And you don't have to spend much cash to make that happen.

Whether you are planning to work in a garage, basement, spare room, or steel shipping container, you probably don't have enough light on hand for building things. Your goal should be nearly enough light to land a plane.

Seriously, though, you'll be surprised at what a difference a flood of light makes. No matter where you are in your workspace, you'll want to see fine print, tiny pencil marks, sanding scratches, and dripping finishes.

But don't fret, lights are cheap if you keep it simple. Good old-fashioned fluorescent fixtures are $12 to $20 each at the home center. Spend the $20 and you'll get fixtures that run quieter and work in colder temps without flickering. The long fluorescent bulbs ("lamps") will run you another $3 to $5 each. If your ceilings are low, consider getting fixtures with covers, to protect the bulbs from an accidental blow with a long board or pipe clamp.

Basic fluorescent shop lights have standard cords and plugs, so you or an electrician just need to add a few extra outlets to the ceiling and connect them to a switch. Or you can wire together all the fixtures and avoid the dangling power cords.

An even greener option is 100-watt LED bulbs, which screw into standard porcelain light fixtures. Again, you or your local electrician will need to do some basic wiring to mount lots of these fixtures on the ceiling, but LED bulbs throw color-correct light, plus they last much longer and cost less than fluorescent tubes in the long run. That said, the LED

GEARING UP: WHERE TO BUILD AND WHAT TO BUILD WITH

DON'T STRUGGLE IN DIM LIGHT. The easiest way to add a flood of light to your shop is to hang fluorescent strip lights (far left), which plug into normal outlets. If you can wire in some plain porcelain light bases, you can use long-lasting, energy-saving 100-watt LED bulbs (above). You'll need a few more of those than you'll need fluorescent tubes (left).

approach will be a little spendier than fluorescent fixtures, lumen for lumen (a measure of light).

let there be heat, too

You don't need your workspace to be at a steady 68 degrees year-round, but keeping it between 55 and 80 will be much more pleasant. Also, below 55 degrees, some wood glues and wood finishes won't dry properly.

It isn't hard to warm or cool a small space enough to be comfortable. You can cool down by opening a window, obviously, or using an air conditioner, but the more common problem is cold, especially north of the Mason–Dixon line.

If you are in a basement, spare room, or attached garage, you're halfway home, literally, as you'll soak up some warmth from the living spaces. Do as much insulating and weather-sealing as you can (or want to), and then try one of those electric oil-filled portable heaters. They do a nice job of warming up a small space, and at $40 or $50 at your local home center or department store, you can afford two if need be. They shut off temporarily when they get too hot, which is a nice safety feature.

For more extreme cold or bigger spaces, there are a number of other good solutions. My favorite is a direct-vent propane furnace that mounts on an exterior wall. They have a sealed burner, so wood dust is not an issue. Friends of mine in Southern states have installed very efficient wall-mounted heat pumps (like the units in hotels) that both heat and cool as needed, using electrical power.

The most romantic choice is a wood stove, which also eats up scrapwood. When I lived in New England, I had an old wood stove in my detached woodshop, and I loved the process of making a fire and feeding it during the snowy months as I enjoyed a Zen-like session of building things.

A LITTLE WARMTH FOR LESS. If your shop feels like an oven or a freezer, you'll be less likely to spend time there. An oil-filled electric heater is a cheap and safe way to bring your basement or garage up to a more comfy temperature. At under $50 each, you can afford two. Make sure yours has an automatic shutoff to prevent overheating.

CHOOSING TOOLS: HOW TO DO MORE WITH LESS

This is where I part company with traditional woodworking books, which prepare you to be an old-school fine woodworker. If that's where you want to wind up, this book will give you a great start. But what I love about the Maker movement is that it threw out the old rules. My philosophy for beginners does the same thing.

You don't have to start your woodworking hobby by collecting a bunch of handplanes, handsaws, and fine chisels; learning to sharpen and use them; buying or making a big, traditional workbench; and then tackling the classic wood joints—as if you are an apprentice in a dark workshop in the 18th century.

I think it's more fun to start building projects right away. That's why I recommend using off-the-shelf building materials and a minimal tool set—mostly power tools—at least at first. The downside is noise, but a pair of earmuffs solves that, and the upside is having some early success, building your confidence, and having awesome projects to brag about as soon as possible.

Don't get me wrong, you'll love hand tools after you get through their learning curve, and they will definitely add some fun and refinement to your hobby, but I just wouldn't start there. All of my essential power tools are great for beginners and veterans alike, and they will help you work on your house or apartment for years to come.

Making things even easier, not every part of your project needs to be made of wood. Anything you can find in a home center or hardware store is fair game to build with—be that plastic, metal, or wood—as long as it will look good and last. To take these projects to the next level, I also took advantage of the Internet, which brings a world of curiosities to your door.

Approaching woodworking this way, without any rules, means you won't need complex joints to hold pieces together. In most cases, you can do it with screws, bolts, dowels, and creativity.

BUILD 100 PROJECTS WITH 11 TOOLS

By using off-the-shelf lumber and supplies, you can avoid expensive woodworking machines like a tablesaw and planer. The following tools (OK, a few more than 11 if you count every little thing) will pay for themselves many times over as you do projects and remodeling jobs for years to come. And they are compact enough to fit into your Mini Cooper when you move cross-country.

- Miter saw
- Circular saw
- Jigsaw
- Impact driver and bits
- Small router
- Combination square
- Measuring tape
- Metal rule
- Compass
- Hammer, screwdriver, and other handyman tools
- Wood clamps

MITER SAW IS WORTH THE MONEY. This tool quickly and surely cuts any board to any length at a perfect 90 degrees (or any other angle). Save money with a non-sliding version that only tips over for bevel cuts in one direction, but go for a 12-in. blade (vs. 10-in.) so you can cut wider boards.

THE HUMBLE CIRCULAR SAW. You'll need one of these for wide cuts in plywood. Team it up with the shopmade saw guide in the next chapter and you'll be amazed at what it can do.

JUST ONE MORE. The first two saws can't do curves, but a jigsaw can. Go for contractor quality and it will cut faster and smoother and more accurately.

three saws

You can build most of the projects in this book with just four or five power tools, and believe it or not, one is not a tablesaw—at least not at first. A tablesaw is great for precise cuts of all kinds, including specialized joints, but a decent one will run you $500 at least, and there is a learning curve if you want to stay safe. So I'll save the tablesaw for my next book.

There are three saws I think you do need, and all are pretty simple to use. The first is a *miter saw,* sometimes called a chopsaw. It does one thing really well, which is cut wood to precise lengths, at any angle. Team that up with "presurfaced" lumber, which is already cut to width and thickness, and you can build dozens of projects.

There are pricey sliding miter saws that glide forward and back and tilt in both directions, but I recommend a non-sliding model that tilts just one way and simply chops straight down through a board. It's a breeze to use, and you can get one with a big 12-in. blade for under $250. That will be your biggest expense in this book, but this tool will pay dividends for a lifetime. By the way, I'll give some general price ranges, but you almost always get a better tool if you spend a bit more.

With a miter saw, unlike a tablesaw, the workpiece stays put while the saw moves. So all you have to do is keep your fingers clear and your earmuffs on. If you ever decide to install wood flooring, or build a deck, or add some nice trim inside the house, the chopsaw will be your best friend. Chopsaws are portable, so they can go anywhere the job is, though it's nice to give the saw a permanent home in your workshop, set up and ready to go.

CORDLESS DRILL ON STEROIDS. Don't buy a cordless drill—get an impact driver. This compact 20-volt version can drive the longest screws and drill the deepest holes. The magical impact action means it won't strip screw heads or torque your wrist like a big drill will.

SPECIAL BITS. An impact driver takes only drill and screwdriver bits with hex-shaped shanks.

For wider, longer cuts of all kinds, especially on plywood and other sheet goods, get a *circular saw*, the kind carpenters use, with a 7¼-in. blade. The more you spend on it, the smoother it will cut, but you shouldn't have to spend more than $80. I got mine for $60.

A circular saw can be hard to steer perfectly straight, but we'll turn it into a foolproof track-guided saw with a simple shopmade guide in the next chapter, just one of the many ways you can do much more with less.

And last, for cutting curves, you'll need a *jigsaw*, also $80 or less. Arm it with a long blade designed to make smooth cuts in wood, and you'll be surprised at how well the saw will follow a line and how clean it will cut. I like the saws with built-in LEDs that make it easier to see your pencil line as you cut.

best drill in the biz

My last power-tool recommendation is my favorite tool in the shop, an impact driver, a special kind of cordless drill that is a joy to use. For an extra $80 or so over a standard drill, you can get a compact 12- or

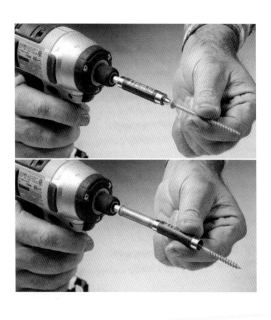

GET A BIT HOLDER FOR DRIVING SCREWS

Also called a screw guide, a bit holder holds different driver bits for all different types of screws. It extends your reach so you can drive screws in tight places. The holder has a collar that pulls out around the screw to keep it in line as you drive it. It works great.

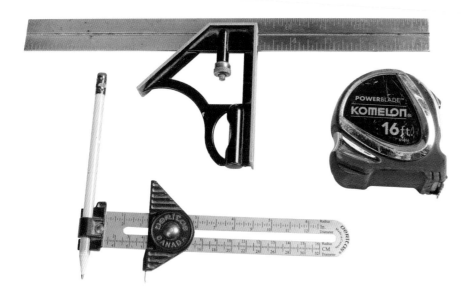

A FEW TOOLS FOR MARKING AND MEASURING. Layout is everything, and these tools will help you do it precisely. Use a combo square to make precise layout marks and check 90-degree angles. A measuring tape measures over long distances. A 4-ft. aluminum straightedge can draw straight lines and be flexed to draw curved ones. And you'll need a compass of some kind (mine is fancy) for small arcs.

20-volt model that will drive the longest screws with ease. What's cool about an impact driver is the vibrating action that kicks in when the going gets tough. These staccato impacts make this small tool much stronger, so it can drive big bolts and screws without stressing your wrist or stripping the head of the screw. Trust me, it's amazing.

Impact drivers work just as well for drilling, but they have a quick-change chuck that only accepts hex-shank drill bits. For a few more bucks you can get a special chuck that will fit into an impact driver and hold standard round shanks, letting you use more types of bits.

a shop vacuum is nice

For general cleanup, and to attach directly to some of your power tools, a shop vacuum is a great idea. If you plan on buying a random-orbit sander (see Chapter 6), you'll definitely need a vac to keep it working well and to keep dust out of your airways.

Shop vacuums are available at all price ranges, with pricier models offering HEPA-level filtration, a

self-cleaning feature that unclogs the filters and keeps suction strong, and an onboard tool outlet that turns on the vac automatically when you turn on the sander, chopsaw, or whatever. Like all tool choices, you can get as geeky as you like.

add a few hand tools for layout

For measuring and marking, which is the critical first stage of any project, you'll need a few essential hand tools. After a sharp pencil, the most important is a combination square, with a sliding 12-in. ruler. As you'll see in this book, you'll use that square to mark workpieces accurately in all sorts of ways, as well as to make sure your finished cuts and assemblies are coming out square.

To make measurements larger than 12 in., you need a tape measure. Almost any one will do, but look for one that reaches at least 12 ft. I also like having a long metal ruler for drawing long, straight lines. I have a 4-ft. aluminum straightedge I got at the home center for $8. As you'll see, I also flex it to draw long, graceful arcs.

SAFETY GEAR: THE MOST IMPORTANT TOOL OF ALL

With all this hot talk about cool tools, I almost forgot the two most important pieces of gear in my workspace: eye and ear protection. With power tools, both of these are a must at all times.

Although ears take longer to hurt than eyes, which can be permanently damaged in an instant, ears lose their power in a cumulative way that is just as irreversible. And the loud bang of a hammer or air nailer can be just as destructive as the prolonged roar of your new miter saw.

The good news is that ear protection, in the form of earmuffs, is cheap, light, and effective. Get a couple of pairs in case you misplace one. Earplugs can also be a good choice, but only if you bother to roll them up and stick them in properly each time you need them. And even then, most muffs offer better protection. Another cool thing about earmuffs is how easy it is to build in Bluetooth®, so you can listen to talk or tunes while you do something tedious. Just be careful that your death metal or pan flute isn't distracting.

As for eye protection, you can probably get by with everyday prescription glasses if you wear them, but make sure the lenses are shatterproof polycarbonate. That said, real safety glasses are the best bet. They hug your face more closely, helping to ward off little projectiles that might bounce up and in. You can get safety glasses with prescription lenses if you don't want to trust your everyday glasses.

Thanks to my friend Chris Gardner, editor of two awesome DIY websites, ManMadeDIY.com and curbly.com, for standing in as my safety model.

SAFETY GLASSES DON'T HAVE TO BE NERDY. Look for glasses that hug your face closely and are comfortable to wear.

EARMUFFS ARE QUICK AND TRUSTWORTHY. Look for soft padding inside, so they hug your head without gaps.

READY TO ROLL. With your eyes and ears protected, you'll have peace of mind. Just remember to keep your fingers safe.

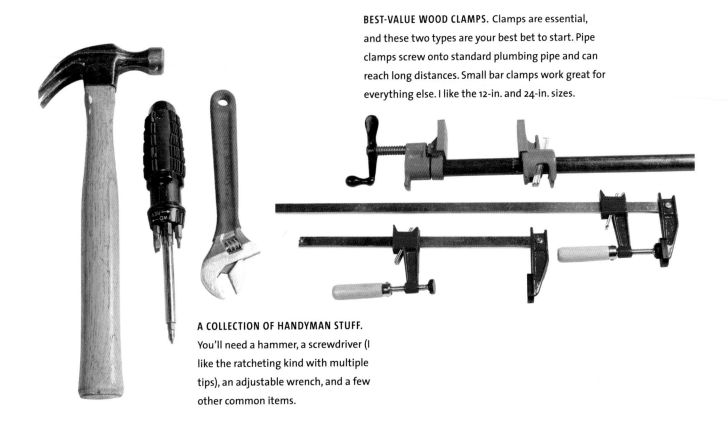

BEST-VALUE WOOD CLAMPS. Clamps are essential, and these two types are your best bet to start. Pipe clamps screw onto standard plumbing pipe and can reach long distances. Small bar clamps work great for everything else. I like the 12-in. and 24-in. sizes.

A COLLECTION OF HANDYMAN STUFF. You'll need a hammer, a screwdriver (I like the ratcheting kind with multiple tips), an adjustable wrench, and a few other common items.

To draw tighter circles and arcs, get a compass of some kind. I have a cool one called a Veritas® Carpenter's Gauge, from LeeValley.com, but a standard drawing compass will work fine. Watch out for the online retailers like Lee Valley®, Rockler®, and Woodcraft®. You might be drawn into their powerful vortexes and never be seen again.

Beyond that, you'll need some standard handyman tools, like a hammer, screwdrivers, adjustable wrench, and such. Buy them as you need them. As always, avoid the cheapest models. Buy decent tools and they will be your friends for life.

clamp it!

Last but not least, they say a woodworker can never have enough clamps. I disagree. There are tons of types, and if you end up deep into fine furniture making, you might need them all. But for everything you will build in this book, and 90% of what you will most likely make in the future, you can rely on just one type: an F-style bar clamp. These are lightweight, easy to use, and can put pinpoint pressure wherever you need it. Once again, buy quality. I went for the medium-duty bar clamps, called "economy standard fast-acting clamps" at LeeValley.com, in two sizes, 12 in. and 24 in. Get at least four of each.

You'll also see a couple of wooden hand screws pop up in later chapters. They are not a must, but they are old-timey and come in handy, as you'll see.

And though I don't use them in this book, I recommend having a few pipe clamps. These are actually attachments that screw onto any length of plumbing pipe. And that's their strength: They can reach as far as you need them to. Put them on some 3-ft. or 4-ft. lengths of pipe for easy handling, and then you can always buy longer pipe for special jobs.

Affordability, quality, and versatility equal value, and I'm all about value. There is something beautiful about just enough.

ALL ABOUT WOOD

Wood comes in a few different forms. To start with there is solid lumber, straight from the tree; then there are man-made sheet goods: plywood and MDF (medium-density fiberboard, which is flat, hard, and handy). Let's start with the solid stuff.

First off, solid wood starts off roughsawn, and for some species that's the only way to get it. But you should stick with boards that have already been surfaced for you, so you don't need an expensive jointer and planer to mill them flat and straight.

Second, wood moves—that is to say it expands and contracts with seasonal moisture changes. The key is that it barely changes along its length, but it does shrink and expand across the grain, changing slightly in thickness and quite a bit in width. The amount of humidity change varies by region, but no matter where you live, you have to factor in some wood movement when designing with wood.

Here's a common predicament: Picture a wide board, lying flat, meeting another board at a right angle, as in a frame of some kind. One board will stay the same along its length, while the width of the other will change. See the problem, especially if the boards are very wide? Wood movement won't be a factor for most of our projects, but for a few it will, and I'll get into it then.

As for plywood and MDF, they don't expand or contract to speak of, and they tend to be flatter than solid wood and stay that way, all properties we will take advantage of in this book.

where to get it

As for where to get wood, the home center or large-scale hardware store will have a nice selection of presurfaced solid wood, from deck boards to premium hardwoods, plus project parts of all sorts of shapes and sizes. I take full advantage of those in this book.

The prices are especially good at home centers, but you might have to pick through the boards to find ones that are straight and undamaged. Beyond the home center, there's the lumberyard, which often includes a big hardware store and boasts an even bigger selection of deck boards and hardwoods. The wood quality is also a step up from the home center, but so are the prices. What's also great about home centers and big hardware stores is all the other stuff you can find, like screws, bolts, pipes, and other things to build with.

Fewer and farther between you'll find hardwood dealers, which have scores of wood species from around the world, as well as some specialty plywoods that can be pretty cool. I head to the hardwood store in this book too, though I avoid the really pricey stuff there.

In general, if you stick with woods that grow in your region, you'll save a lot of money, avoiding the cost of shipping it across the country or ocean even.

Some people like to work with reclaimed wood—old flooring, barn boards, and such—and that's great if you can find boards that suit your purpose and you want that rustic, reclaimed look. But you'll probably need a tablesaw to cut reclaimed wood to the widths you need, and a planer to change its thickness or flatten rough surfaces. And then you might end up hitting a nail and needing a new blade for your machine. But it can be worth the trouble.

As for plywood and MDF, the home center once again has fewer varieties than the lumberyard, but better prices. A hardwood retailer will have even more, and like the lumberyard will be happy to order special types that they don't have on hand.

don't be afraid to ask questions

You might feel awkward the first time you go into a lumberyard or hardwood store, but remember that the good folks there want to sell you wood, and they want repeat customers. So there are no dumb questions.

Asking questions can also get you wood from unexpected sources. For the desk in Chapter 7, I wanted a big, thick slab, with the natural, wavy bark edges still on it. I know that some specialty hardwood suppliers keep big slabs on hand, but they sell those mostly to pros, who don't mind paying a lot and passing that on to their clients.

On the other hand, private citizens sometimes have slabs they are happy to unload. So I reached out to my local woodworking club, the Guild of Oregon Woodworkers, and asked if they knew anyone with slabs to sell. Sure enough, someone suggested a local pro, and I told him what I was looking for with a quick phone call. He had just the thing on hand and sold it at less than half the price the local hardwood retailers would have charged.

Get involved in your local woodworking club or Maker space, and you'll start making connections, getting inspired, hearing about great deals, and gaining access to tools you don't have at home.

Like I said in the last chapter, the key is diving in. So enough talk—let's build something.

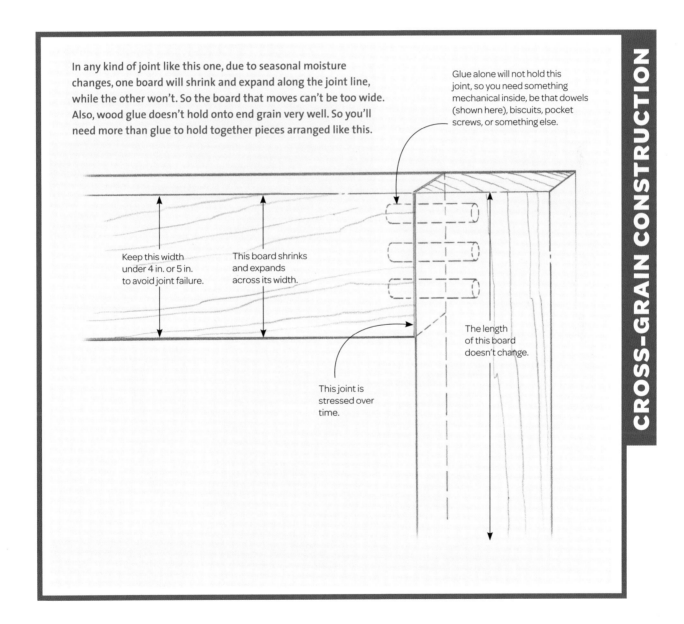

In any kind of joint like this one, due to seasonal moisture changes, one board will shrink and expand along the joint line, while the other won't. So the board that moves can't be too wide. Also, wood glue doesn't hold onto end grain very well. So you'll need more than glue to hold together pieces arranged like this.

Glue alone will not hold this joint, so you need something mechanical inside, be that dowels (shown here), biscuits, pocket screws, or something else.

Keep this width under 4 in. or 5 in. to avoid joint failure.

This board shrinks and expands across its width.

The length of this board doesn't change.

This joint is stressed over time.

CROSS-GRAIN CONSTRUCTION

FINDING LUMBER

I got 90 percent of the supplies for this book at my local home center and the rest from a variety of other sources, from hardwood dealers to the far reaches of the Interwebs.

BIG-BOX HOME CENTERS ARE PACKED WITH GREAT VALUES AND INSPIRATION. Deck boards (bottom left) are great for outdoor projects, there is always a selection of hardwoods (right), plus there are lots of miscellaneous supplies, like these superwide pine project boards (bottom right) and small parts and pieces (below).

LUMBERYARDS ARE GREAT, TOO. Your local contractor lumberyard will usually have a nice selection of presurfaced hardwoods, plus all the material you can get at the home center. Make sure boards are straight before bringing them home.

HARDWOOD DEALERS HAVE EVEN BETTER BOARDS. Hardwood retailers are a candy store of woods from around the world. As a beginner you should look for presurfaced boards. If they don't have them on hand, they'll be glad to surface their roughsawn boards for you, for a small charge.

2

two projects to supercharge your workspace

I'M DEFINITELY NOT in the group that tries to perfect their workshops before building anything substantial, but a little preparation goes a long way. So let's compromise. Let's start building right away, but start with two easy projects that will make your workspace work harder. Better yet, the first small project will help you make the second one.

Every workshop needs a few solid surfaces to work on. At some point in the future, you might want to build or buy a true workbench with a basic woodworking vise on it for holding work quickly and securely. But for now—for all the projects in this book in fact—all you really need is a small workstation with valuable storage built in. My time-saving move here will be to use a kitchen cabinet as the core, putting a sturdy surface on top and wheels below, so you can roll it into a corner when you don't need it.

Small surplus cabinets are easy to find—I found this one for $100 at my local Habitat for Humanity® ReStore—but a kitchen cabinet is not quite ready for prime time, so we'll pimp this one out using an extra 2×4, a good set of casters, a quart of paint, and a sheet of MDF (medium-density fiberboard).

Before we get started, to help you tame that 4×8 sheet of MDF—and all the plywood to come—we'll build one of my favorite shop helpers, a saw guide. A saw guide turns any circular saw into an idiot-proof, precision cutting tool. Some folks call a shopmade helper like this a "jig." Throw that word around and you'll sound pretty hardcore.

1

simple saw guide is a plywood champion

You can make this simple but amazing guide for your circular saw from two 2-ft. by 4-ft. pieces of MDF, one thick and one thin, both available at any home center. It will do almost everything a big tablesaw will do, delivering straight cuts in any material, in any direction, right on your layout marks every time. The fence guides the saw, and the edge of the base shows exactly where the blade will cut.

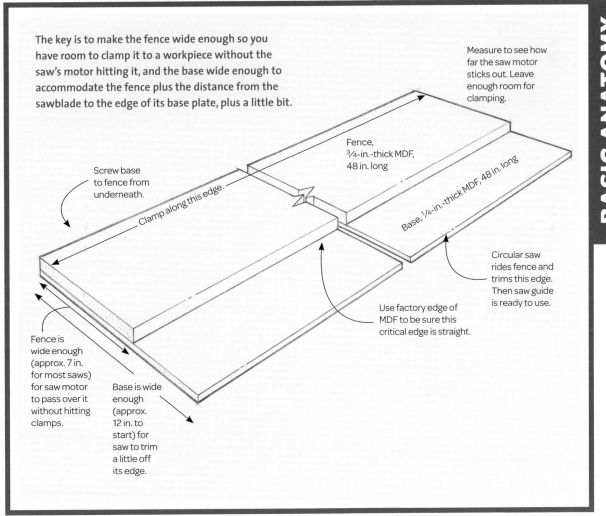

BASIC ANATOMY

The key is to make the fence wide enough so you have room to clamp it to a workpiece without the saw's motor hitting it, and the base wide enough to accommodate the fence plus the distance from the sawblade to the edge of its base plate, plus a little bit.

Measure to see how far the saw motor sticks out. Leave enough room for clamping.

Screw base to fence from underneath.

Clamp along this edge.

Fence, ¾-in.-thick MDF, 48 in. long

Base, ¼-in.-thick MDF, 48 in. long

Circular saw rides fence and trims this edge. Then saw guide is ready to use.

Use factory edge of MDF to be sure this critical edge is straight.

Fence is wide enough (approx. 7 in. for most saws) for saw motor to pass over it without hitting clamps.

Base is wide enough (approx. 12 in. to start) for saw to trim a little off its edge.

SMART APPROACH TO A STRAIGHT SAW GUIDE

The keys here are to use the factory edge of the MDF as the working edge of your fence and to make the base wide enough so a little bit will be trimmed off by the saw, showing you exactly where it will cut in the future.

1 MEASURE YOUR SAW. The key dimension is the distance between the blade and the inside edge of the base plate. **2 CUT THE BASE.** This cut isn't critical, so just draw a line 12 in. away from the edge and cut along it. Set the blade at least $\frac{1}{2}$ in. deep to cut through this $\frac{1}{4}$-in.-thick panel. Notice the foam insulation under the workpiece. That is a great way to support plywood and MDF safely while protecting the table below. Clamp the workpiece to keep it from moving. **3 NOW CUT THE FENCE.** This cut isn't critical either, as I'll be using the dead-straight factory edge (closest to my body here) as the critical edge that guides the saw. **4 DRILL CLEARANCE HOLES.** Notice that I drew a line where the edge of the fence will be, so I know where the screws need to go. This is the lower side of the saw guide, so the holes also need to be countersunk so the screws end up flush and the whole thing will sit flat.

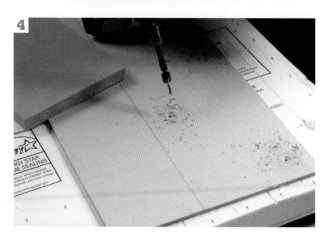

5 THE FEEL TRICK. A clearance hole lets a screw pass through freely. To find a drill bit that is the same size as a screw, just roll the two in your fingers and trust your fingertips. **6 COMBO DRILL/COUNTERSINK.** You can drill and countersink separately, or use a combo bit like this one. **7 PILOT HOLES, TOO.** Clamp the base onto the fence and use the bigger holes to guide you as you drill skinnier pilot holes into the fence below. The tape flag helps me avoid drilling through the fence and scarring my gorgeous creation.

THE SECRET TO SUPER-STRONG SCREWS

Drill the right-size clearance holes and pilot holes, and your screws will be incredibly strong. A countersink at the top lets the screw heads sit flat.

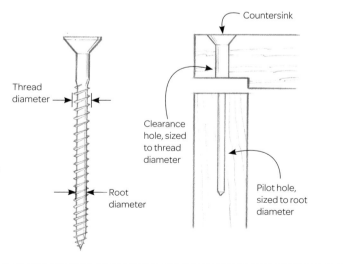

Countersink

Thread diameter

Root diameter

Clearance hole, sized to thread diameter

Pilot hole, sized to root diameter

8 SCREWS WORK PERFECTLY NOW. They clear the base completely and grab the fence below, pulling the two pieces together tightly. Using the countersink bit earlier means that the screw heads are set slightly below the surface.

9 TRIM BEFORE USING. When building the jig, leave a little extra to be trimmed off. Then, once you make that cut, the edge of the guide shows you exactly where the saw will cut in the future, every time.

A HANDY LEVER

Sometimes it helps to raise the saw guard a bit to start a cut, rather than letting the workpiece push it out of the way. Do that by pushing forward on that lever near the top of the saw.

build a rolling workstation

I found this surplus cabinet for $100, painted its sides, and added a thick top and casters to create a mobile workstation for my miter saw, with handy storage inside. This is the only workbench you need to start building projects. Make the top overhang the sides and you'll be able to clamp things to it easily. Then you can pull out one of your tools from below and go to work.

KITCHEN CABINET PLUS

Start with a standard kitchen cabinet (surplus models are cheap) and add a thick top and a rolling base to make a mobile workbench.

1 CUT THE BASE AND TOP PIECES. Use your trusty saw guide here. You need only one mark at each end of the cut, then you can just line up the guide, clamp it down, and cut. Note the foamboard below again, supporting the workpiece and protecting your worktable.

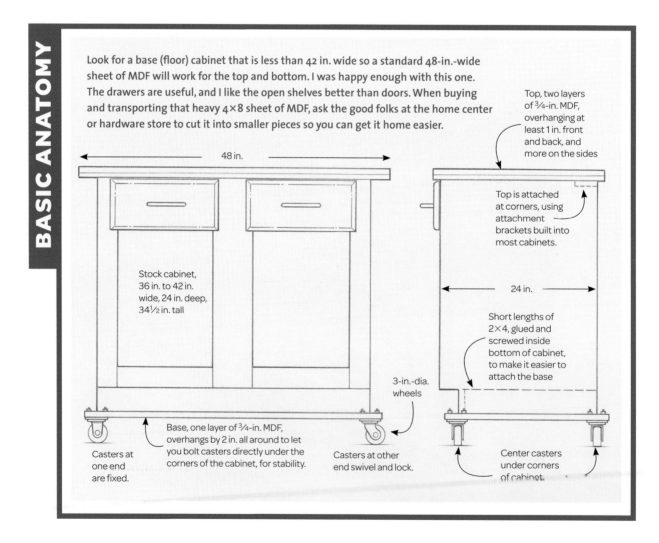

BASIC ANATOMY

Look for a base (floor) cabinet that is less than 42 in. wide so a standard 48-in.-wide sheet of MDF will work for the top and bottom. I was happy enough with this one. The drawers are useful, and I like the open shelves better than doors. When buying and transporting that heavy 4×8 sheet of MDF, ask the good folks at the home center or hardware store to cut it into smaller pieces so you can get it home easier.

48 in.

Stock cabinet, 36 in. to 42 in. wide, 24 in. deep, 34½ in. tall

3-in.-dia. wheels

Casters at one end are fixed.

Base, one layer of ¾-in. MDF, overhangs by 2 in. all around to let you bolt casters directly under the corners of the cabinet, for stability.

Casters at other end swivel and lock.

Top, two layers of ¾-in. MDF, overhanging at least 1 in. front and back, and more on the sides

Top is attached at corners, using attachment brackets built into most cabinets.

24 in.

Short lengths of 2×4, glued and screwed inside bottom of cabinet, to make it easier to attach the base

Center casters under corners of cabinet.

2 MAKE THE TOP TWO LAYERS THICK. Do that by screwing up through the bottom layer into the top one (both are flipped over here). Drywall screws ($1\frac{1}{4}$ in.) work just fine. Just drill clearance holes in the bottom layer for the screws to pass through, and countersink those holes. I used my combo drill/countersink bit here. You don't need pilot holes in the top layer (bottom in this photo).   **3 FLIP THE CABINET AND MOUNT THE TOP.** Lay the benchtop on the floor, top side down, place the cabinet on it upside down, and measure at the edges to even out the overhang. Almost all kitchen cabinets have a way to screw them to a countertop. If yours doesn't, or you don't think it is strong enough, you might need to glue and screw on some extra strips around the top of the cabinet (while the cabinet is right side up), as we are about to do for the base.   **4 IMPROVE THE BASE OF THE CABINET.** To screw a base and casters onto the bottom of a cabinet with thin sides, you need to reinforce it a bit. Do that by cutting some 2×4s to fit into the outside edges, brushing a thick layer of wood glue onto them, and screwing through the outsides of the cabinet to attach them. Again, use clearance holes and countersink them. Hold the wood pieces level with the bottom of the cabinet as you drive the screws.

5

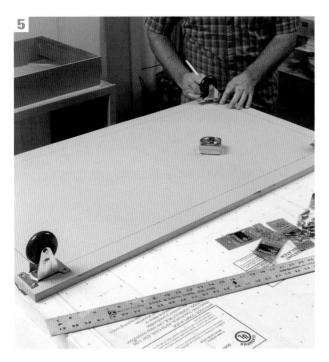

6

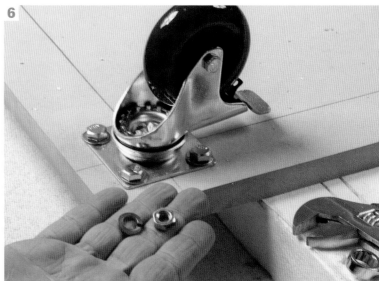

7

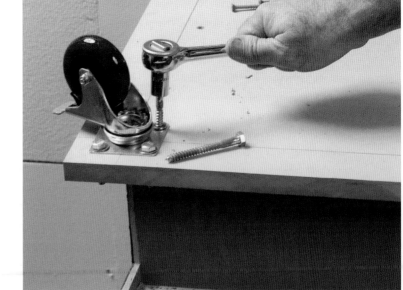

5 LOCATE THE CASTERS ON THE BASE PLATE. Cut another big piece of MDF, 2 in. bigger than the bottom of the cabinet all around, so you can bolt on the casters. Draw lines to indicate the outline of the cabinet, and center the casters on the corners of the cabinet as you mark the locations for the bolt holes. Then drill those. **6 USE LOCK WASHERS.** The tops of the bolts get normal flat washers but the nut sides gets lock washers. Bolt through the three outside holes but not the inside one right now. **7 LAST HOLE GETS A LAG BOLT.** Place the base-and-caster assembly onto the cabinet bottom. The inside hole on each caster now gets a lag bolt (a big, thick wood screw with a hex head on it), driven down into those 2×4s you just attached. You've already got bolt holes in the base, but you need to drill pilot holes into the 2×4s below for the lag bolts. And just to be sure the base is attached securely, also drive some drywall or decking screws into the 2×4s below.

CASTERS 101 Urethane tires are best, at least 3 in. in diameter. The best arrangement for workshop casters is two fixed ones and two swivel casters with brakes. These will let you wheel the cabinet around the shop and into tight corners, but be more stable than using four swivel casters.

SIMPLE WORK SUPPORT FOR THE MITER SAW

It helps a lot to have some sort of support that's level with the base of your miter saw so that long pieces stay stable when you cut them. Here's an easy way to make one using a single 2×4 and a few screws.

SAFER SAWING. To help keep long boards level, screw a couple of lengths of 2×4 together, and then add screws at the bottom corners (right) to fine-tune the height.

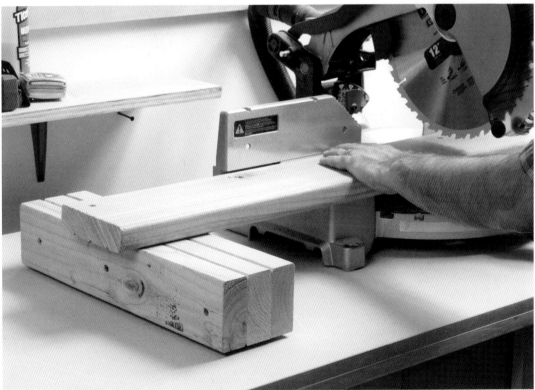

3

party supplies

I KNOW WE SHOULD SAVE

the party for the end, but let's make the journey fun from the beginning. A bottle opener and cornhole game are two party fixtures that will come in handy for years of good living. Everyone knows that uncapping bottles is fun, especially if they are filled with tasty craft beer, or maybe a gourmet cola with cane sugar. But if you don't know about cornhole, you are missing out on a great backyard game, one that dominates the tailgate scene these days. It's a lot like lawn darts, without the potential for maiming the neighbor's kid.

I'm not going to comment on the name of the game, other than to say that it derives from the bags of dry corn that are pitched into said hole. That said, it's fun to announce loudly at church gatherings, "Let's play cornhole!"

Like most of the projects in this book, both of these party accessories are easily made from the ocean of supplies that await you at the home center. I've seen bottle-opener hardware there too, but I went online to find just the opener I wanted, as well as the super-magnet that turns the project into a party trick (see below).

CAP CATCHER. Pop the top and let the cap drop. It stops in midair below, sticking to your favorite message, or logo, or whatever you want to glue on. The secret is a big rare earth magnet, buried in the back of the board.

PROJECT N°.

magic bottle opener

Go online and you'll find all sorts of bottle openers, from vintage to sports-themed. You'll even find little cups that sit below to catch the caps, with both items screwing easily to any chunk of wood. To make the uncapping even more unbelievable, I borrowed a trick I found in a few places online. By burying a rare earth magnet in the back of the board, you can make the falling caps jump onto the wood in a mysterious cluster.

I took it up one more notch by placing the logo of my favorite sports team where the caps collect. I shaped the board to fit that logo, but many logos are generally round so this shape should work for most of them. If your favorite logo, or Chinese character, or ironic picture of a reviled political character isn't round, I trust you will shape the board accordingly.

BASIC ANATOMY

Place opener where it looks best to you.

1⅞-in. radius

Draw light centerline on front and back.

7 in. between center points

Back board, any wood, approx. ¾ in. thick and at least 12 in. long by 6 in. wide

Rare earth magnet

4-in. circle (Light pencil line guides sticker placement.)

Shallow 1⅜-in.-dia. hole holds magnet.

Outside edge is 3-in. radius.

LAYOUT IS EVERYTHING

I borrowed this phrase from my friend Marc Adams, who runs the biggest woodworking school in North America. It also happens to be a fact.

SUPPLIES

- Starr® X bottle opener (available from various online suppliers)
- Rare earth (neodymium) magnet, 35mm (1³⁄₈ in.) by 5mm with countersunk hole (available from various online suppliers)
- Keyhole Fitting—Double, ⁹⁄₁₆ in. by 3 in., item No. 28829 (available from www.rockler.com)

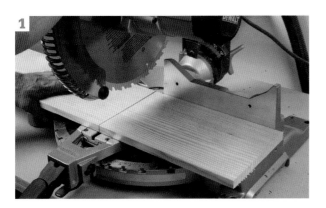

1 CHOP OFF A CHUNK. This wood is hemlock, which is abundant in the Northwest and sold at home centers, but any nice board will do. Chop it to the length you need.
2 CENTERLINES, FRONT AND BACK. Use your combination square to mark a light centerline down the front and back of the board (by measuring the width and dividing in it half). This will help you center all the arcs and hardware. **3 MARK TWO ARCS.** The smaller one goes at the top of the board (see "Basic Anatomy" on the facing page), and the other radius should be 1 in. bigger than your logo sticker, so the wood ends up bordering it nicely. I like my snazzy compass from www.leevalley.com, but any compass will work. **4 CONNECT THE CURVES.** Straight lines complete the perimeter layout. **5 ONE MORE ARC.** This circle is just a hair bigger than the sticker, to help you center it when you stick it on. Draw this arc lightly so it's easy to erase.

CUT AND SMOOTH THE BOARD

A jigsaw handles curves and straight lines just as well.

1 SLOW AND STEADY. Clamp down the workpiece, and stay just outside the line when cutting. Use your inside hand to hold the base of the jigsaw flat on the wood.

JIGSAW BASICS

People often overlook the jigsaw as a serious woodworking tool, waiting until they can afford an expensive bandsaw for cutting curves. But armed with the right blades, the jigsaw can make clean, smooth curves, and straight cuts too.

BUY BETTER BLADES. There are special blades that are designed for clean cuts in wood. They are also longer than standard blades, letting you cut thicker boards.

CHECK THE BASE. Use a small square to lock the base square to the blade. Bonus tip: Make a few practice cuts—straight and curved—to get the hang of the tool.

MAKE YOUR OWN SANDING BLOCK

A sanding block gives you much more control than using your fingers to hold the paper. Any piece of wood will work, but try to size it just a bit narrower than a quarter-sheet of sandpaper.

ROUND THE EDGES OF THE BLOCK. This way the sandpaper won't catch and tear on workpieces and will lie flatter on the block.

TEARING TIP. Fold the paper in half, both ways, to crease it, and then use a metal ruler to tear it cleanly into four pieces.

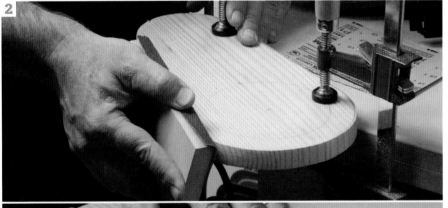

2 SMOOTH THE EDGES. Use a sanding block first with 80-grit paper and then 120-grit paper to sand the edges down to the line (left). Feel with your fingers to see if the curves are even and smooth, and then sand a little bevel on the top and bottom edges (below left).

HIDE THE MAGNET

A big rare earth magnet is buried inside the board, to grab the bottle caps as they fall.

1 MARK THE CENTER POINT. It is centered behind the logo sticker, so it's the same center point you used on top of the board. **2 GRAB A BIG BIT.** A cheaper carpenter's spade bit would work in a soft wood like this, but I went with a Forstner bit I had on hand. It is a 1⅜-in. bit, just a hair larger than the 35mm-dia. magnet. **3 YOU MIGHT NEED THIS CHUCK.** An impact driver only accepts hex-shanked bits, and my 1⅜-in. Forstner bit has a round shank. An auxiliary chuck solves the problem. **4 DRILL AS DEEP AS YOU DARE.** The deeper you go, the better the magnet will work. Use a 1⅜-in. Forstner bit to drill almost through the board. Check the depth frequently to make sure you don't drill through to the front! **5 GLUE IN THE MAGNET.** Super Glue® (cyanoacrylate glue) bonds both wood and metal just as well. Squirt some in, and then press the magnet down into the pocket. **6 STICK ON THE STICKER.** If you look closely, you'll see that faint circle in pencil, which helps me put the sticker in the right spot. **7 SOME STICKERS NEED HELP.** Mine is the moveable vinyl kind, which isn't very sticky. So I sprayed the back first with contact cement, also called spray adhesive or craft spray.

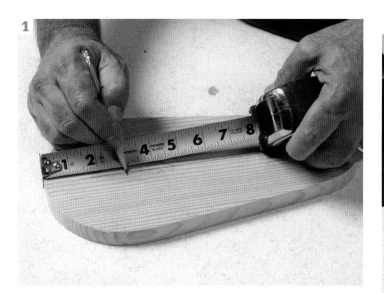

LOCATE THE HARDWARE

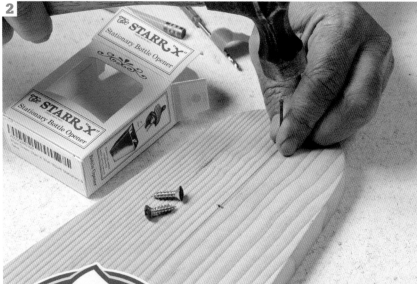

1 **LOCATE THE SCREW HOLES.** Place the bottle opener on the centerline wherever it looks best and mark the centers of the holes. Then flip over the board and place the hanger plate (keyhole fitting) right behind the bottle opener, marking its holes, too.   **2** **PREDRILL.** First use a small nail to make a slight dent at each mark for the drill to follow. For these pilot holes, choose drills a bit smaller than the screws. Add a little tape flag to help you avoid drilling through the board. When the flag brushes the chips away, stop drilling. Love that trick.   **3** **ERASE THE LINES.** Before brushing on the polyurethane finish, erase all the pencil marks and wipe off all the dust.

TWO QUICK COATS OF POLYURETHANE

I'll cover a thicker, more protective version of this finish in Chapter 5, but the bottle opener needs only two coats.

1 BRUSH IT ON. Get some oil-based satin polyurethane, stir it well, and brush it on smoothly with a foam brush. Do the top and edges, let it dry, and then flip the board and finish the back too. **2 SAND AND REPEAT.** Using 220-grit paper, sand the wood areas lightly, wipe off the dust with a paper towel, and brush on one more coat.

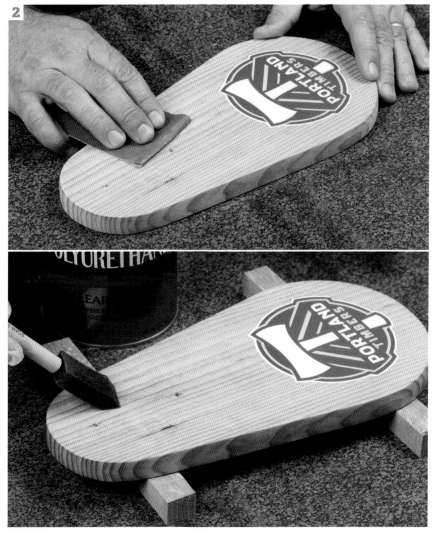

ATTACH THE HARDWARE AND ENJOY

The rest is easy. With the finishing done, the hardware goes on quickly.

1 SCREW ON THE HANGER. This is a double keyhole fitting, for an extra-strong grip. You'll also need to drive two small screws into the wall or side of a cabinet or wherever you want to hang the opener. The keyhole fitting will grab those screws firmly. **2 NOW THE BOTTLE OPENER.** This goes high on the front side, wherever you think it looks right. The pilot holes are already drilled, so the screws go in quickly. **3 SCORE!** The caps get caught every time. It's sure to amaze your friends.

let's play cornhole!

This game is no joke, at least not to the American Cornhole Association (www.playcornhole.org), which has an awesomely serious set of rules and standards for all aspects of the game, including player conduct ("An ACA member, while in competition, shall make no disturbing noises or movements . . . .").

The Web site provides detailed dimensions for the equipment, and I followed those exactly, with one exception. Because we are using off-the-shelf lumber in this book, I had to go with 2½-in.-wide boards for the frame, making it a whopping ½ in. taller than regulations. After you open a few bottles, you won't know the difference.

I added one other twist on the ACA guidelines, one that I don't think they'll mind. I devised a way to attach the two cornhole platforms back to back, so they become a thin suitcase of sorts, with the bean bags thrown in the middle for storage. Portable party, dude.

My other brainstorm was how to cut the big 6-in.-dia. holes in the platform without buying a big, pricey hole saw for this one-off job. Instead, you can do it with the jigsaw you already own, using a nail and a small piece of plywood or MDF. It's your second jig, and it's for your jigsaw. I'll leave it to the etymologists to argue about the relationship between the words.

FUN AT PARTIES AND PICNICS. With this travel-friendly design, you can take the game anywhere and be playing in minutes.

Makes two platforms:

- Two pieces $\frac{1}{2}$-in. plywood, 2 ft. by 4 ft.

- Four $\frac{3}{4}$-in. pine boards, $2\frac{1}{2}$ in. wide by 8 ft. long (width can vary a bit)

- Four carriage bolts, $\frac{3}{8}$ in. by 2 in., with metal washers and lock nuts

- Four plastic washers

- One box #8 deck screws, 2 in. long

- Twelve #8 deck screws, $1\frac{1}{4}$ in. long

- Four window sash locks

- Rope for carry handles, $\frac{1}{2}$ in. thick

- 1 qt. latex paint, glossy (more if you want multiple colors)

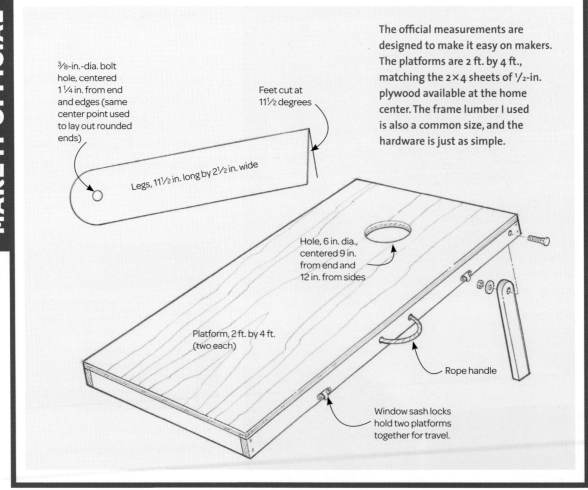

$\frac{3}{8}$-in.-dia. bolt hole, centered $1\frac{1}{4}$ in. from end and edges (same center point used to lay out rounded ends)

Feet cut at $11\frac{1}{2}$ degrees

Legs, $11\frac{1}{2}$ in. long by $2\frac{1}{2}$ in. wide

The official measurements are designed to make it easy on makers. The platforms are 2 ft. by 4 ft., matching the 2×4 sheets of $\frac{1}{2}$-in. plywood available at the home center. The frame lumber I used is also a common size, and the hardware is just as simple.

Hole, 6 in. dia., centered 9 in. from end and 12 in. from sides

Platform, 2 ft. by 4 ft. (two each)

Rope handle

Window sash locks hold two platforms together for travel.

CIRCLE-CUTTER IS A GREAT JIG

You could drill this big hole with a $30 hole saw or do the job for free with a simple little gizmo for your jigsaw. First you need to do some layout and drilling to get ready.

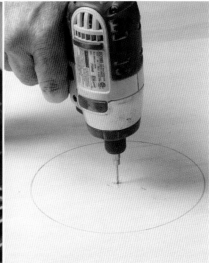

1 LAY OUT THE HOLE. Center it side to side and then measure from the top edge to finish the crisscross (top left). Then draw a 6-in.-dia. circle using any compass you have (top right).
2 DRILL A PERFECT NAIL HOLE. The circle-cutting jig will pivot on a nail, so find a nail and drill bit that match each other (above) and drill a hole at the center point (above right). **3 JIGSAW NEEDS A STARTING POINT.** A ⅜-in. drill bit will work well for most jigsaw blades. You'll need to overlap the outside of the circle by a little to let the jigsaw blade drop in and line up with the circle.

4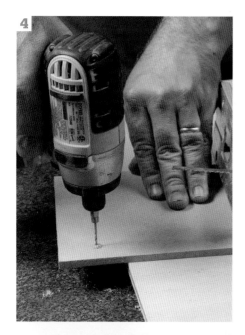

5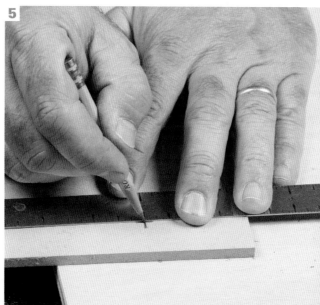

6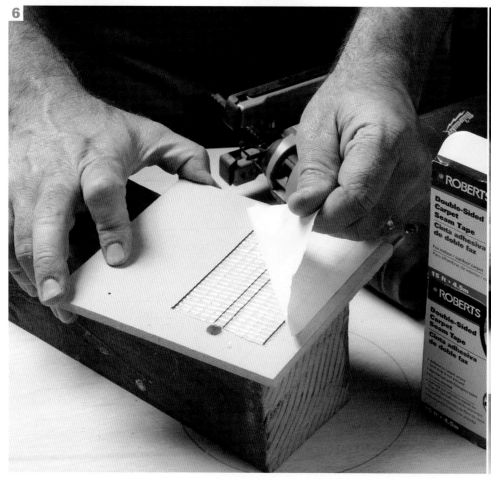

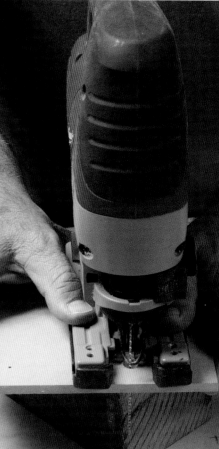

7

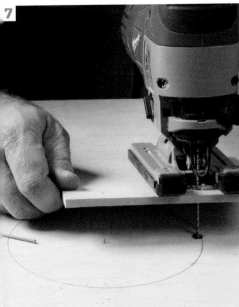 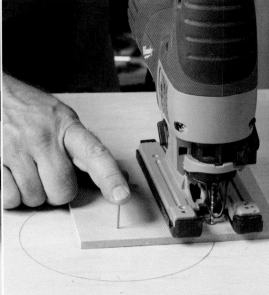 

8

9

4 JIGS NEED A NAIL HOLE TOO. All you need is a thin piece of plywood or MDF for this jig. Start by drilling a hole for the nail. **5 NEXT HOLE SETS THE RADIUS.** Now, at the same distance from the edge as the nail hole and exactly 3 in. away, make center marks and drill a 3/8-in. hole. **6 ATTACHMENT IS CRITICAL.** Double-faced tape is super-handy. Use it to attach the jigsaw to the jig. The key when attaching the jigsaw is to center the blade in the 3/8-in. hole and, at the same time, line the base of the saw up exactly parallel with the end of the jig (perpendicular to the holes) so the sawblade wants to travel straight as it goes around the circle. **7 THIS IS THE FUN PART.** Drop the blade into the hole, press the pivot nail down, and start cutting! Pull back after you go a few inches to make sure the blade isn't wandering off the line. If it is, you'll need to detach the saw and correct its alignment on the jig. **8 DROP THAT DISK.** Go easy at the end for a smooth finish, and watch the disk drop out. You have achieved cornhole! The rest is just window dressing. **9 SAND IT SMOOTH.** Use rough sandpaper to bevel the edge of the circle. Notice the little extra bump from the drilled access hole? Don't worry—no one else will.

MITER SAW BASICS

Although you can cut boards to length with your circular saw, a miter saw makes it much easier. It supports the workpiece and makes accurate cuts at any angle you need. Super-simple to use, it comes in handy for all kinds of projects around the house, like installing moldings or laying an entire floor.

LONG BOARDS TO THE LEFT. If you are a righty, rest long boards on your work support to the left, where you can hold onto them.

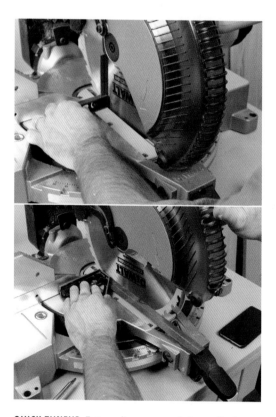

SHORTER END TO THE RIGHT. In this case, this is the piece I am cutting to length, so I make sure my pencil mark is lined up with the right edge of the blade.

QUICK TUNEUP. Every miter saw needs two adjustments. Start by squaring the blade to the table (top), and setting the stop (usually in the back) so the saw always comes back to that position. Then lock the saw into its 90-degree position side to side (bottom) and adjust the plate that brings it back there every time. Check the manual for specifics.

KEEP YOUR HANDS CLEAR. Four in. from the blade is a good rule of thumb (let's keep those thumbs). Hold the workpiece firmly, and just bring the saw down steadily, letting it cut. *Always* wear ear and eye protection with power tools.

SCREW ON THE FRAME

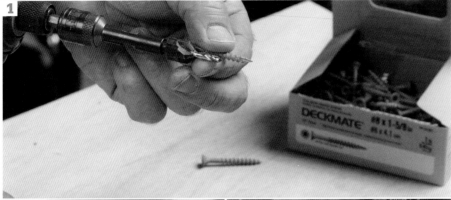

1 DRILL CLEARANCE HOLES IN THE PLATFORM. I'm doing this with a combination drill/countersink bit, which will set the screw heads flush with the surface. The drill bit is just bigger than the screw. Draw some guidelines to show how thick the frame pieces are down below, and consider where the pieces will begin and end when drilling these holes. **2 LONG PIECES FIRST.** Cut these 4 ft. long, clamp them in place, and drill small pilot holes down into them to avoid splitting them. Then drive screws with no worries.

3 TEST-FIT THE SHORT PIECES. Nibble away at these until they drop snugly into place between the long frame pieces, and draw letters on the pieces so you know where they go.

4 SCREW INTO THE ENDS FIRST. Drill clearance holes with the combo bit as before, then position the pieces and drill smaller pilot holes before driving in the screws. This is the sequence for getting maximum holding power from screws without splitting the wood. **5 NOW THE TOP SIDE.** Finally, drive screws down through the platform into the end frame pieces, locking them in place. Be sure to drill those pilot holes first.

BOLT ON THE LEGS

1 LAY OUT THE LEGS. In order to pivot under the platform, the legs need a half-circle cut on their ends. Mark the center points for these curves and then mark them with any compass. **2 DRILL THE LEGS.** To make sure this big 3/8-in. drill bit doesn't wander, first make a dent on your marks using a big nail. Put a piece of scrapwood under the legs when drilling to prevent the drill from chipping out the back side. **3 USE THE LEGS AS A DRILL GUIDE.** To drill matching holes in the frame, position the legs in the corners and drill through them into the frame. Just drill a little bit to mark the spot, and then remove the leg to finish the job.

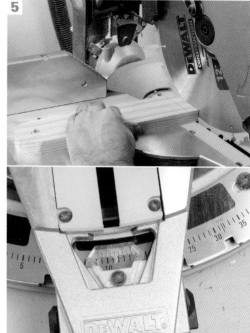

4 SAW THE CURVES. The jigsaw makes short work of these little curves. Just hold the base down on the leg to keep it flat and square to the cut.   **5 CHOP THE ENDS AT AN ANGLE.** This will make the legs sit flat on the ground. You should have already cut them to the right length, so just make the angle end right at the tip. A 11½-degree angle will make them sit flat on the ground.   **6 SMART BOLT SETUP.** Use a ⅜-in. carriage-head bolt, plus a locking nut and two washers, one plastic and one metal. The square head of the carriage bolt will sink into the wood on the back side and resist turning, making it easy to tighten everything in place. The plastic washer goes between the wood parts to reduce friction, and then the leg, metal washer, and lock nut go on. Tighten the nut firmly and it won't come loose.   **7 TEST RUN.** Pivot the legs up into their working position. Note how the curve lets them pivot, and they come to rest tight against the frame.

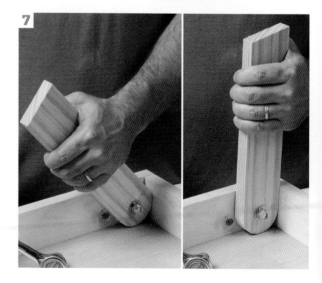

PICK YOUR PAINT JOB

Designing is as fun as building. On any project you build, a little extra time at the design stage will ensure that you'll be happy with the final project. Use any tools at your disposal to do so. In this case, I used the word-processing program on my computer (it has some graphic capabilities) to come up with the paint design for the platforms and then pick colors for the beanbags. Feel free to go with this look, or impress your friends with your own nerdy/ gross/stylish theme.

1 USER-FRIENDLY. Grab some medium-grit sandpaper and your trusty block and knock off the sharp corners. **2 BASE COLOR FIRST.** I started with the blue on the platforms. The first coat will feel fuzzy after it dries, so sand it lightly with fine sandpaper and then apply a second coat for a smooth finish.

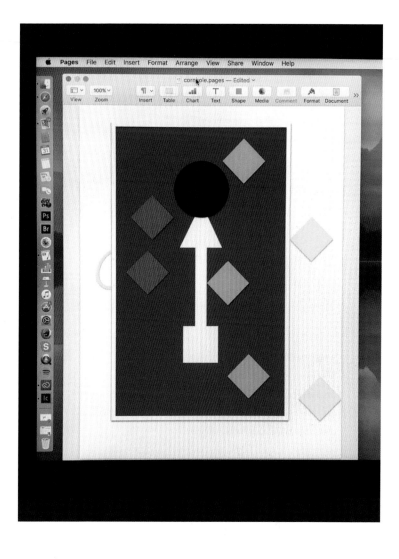

3 LAY OUT YOUR PATTERN. If you want to do more than one color like I did, lay out your next color in pencil and then place wide blue painter's tape outside the lines. Rub the tape with your fingers to be sure it is adhered firmly and paint won't get under it. **4 SLOP ON THE SECOND COLOR.** Just make sure you don't go past the tape, and try to lay it down smoothly. Add a second coat and you are done.
5 PEEL CAREFULLY. Once the paint dries, pull the tape away toward the outside, away from the paint, and go slow and steady. You should get an almost perfect border. It's awesome to see the final pattern emerge.

FINISHING TOUCHES

1 ADD THE ROPE HANDLES. I used ½-in. rope, so I drilled ½-in. holes for it. Then I removed the legs in order to paint them, finished painting the frame, and added the rope handles, knotting the ends. I wrapped the knots with electrical tape to keep them tight. **2 RE-ASSEMBLE.** Bolt the legs back on. The round carriage-bolt heads are cleaner looking then regular bolts. **3 ADD THE WINDOW HARDWARE.** I used window sash locks to hold the two platforms together for storage and travel. Get the strongest ones you can find; these are a bit wimpy. Clamp the two platforms together and hold the hardware in place while you drill pilot holes and drive screws. Space the parts as far apart as you can so they grab firmly when closed.

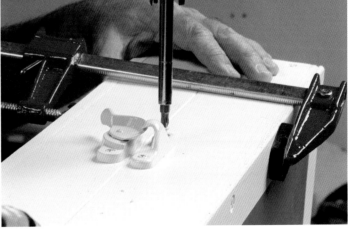

4.

head outdoors with cedar

OUTDOOR PROJECTS are fun to build because things don't have to look as polished as they do inside. And as people have come to embrace the therapeutic value of the big wide world outside their doors, their living spaces have spilled out onto decks, patios, and porches.

No matter where you live, you probably have a spot for a little outdoor oasis. A small bench and a couple of planter boxes are really all you need. Even a big backyard needs a few defined places to sit and reflect.

In fact, you get two benches in this chapter, one stand-alone and the other suspended between planter boxes. I love options, so the planter boxes also work well on their own, chopped a bit shorter and placed wherever they'll fit.

Before we dive into the how-to, let's talk about the wood we'll be using for everything in this chapter. It's one of my favorites.

WHY CEDAR?

This book is all about using materials you can find at any home center or local lumberyard, and cedar is available almost everywhere in the country. Better yet, because it is sold for both deck material (posts, rails, decking, etc.) and fence boards, it comes in all sorts of sizes, both roughsawn and smooth-milled. Still better, cedar isn't that pricey, it's easy to cut and screw into, it's lightweight yet strong, it weathers to a beautiful silvery grey, and like all good outdoor woods, it will resist rot for decades.

As a bonus, cedar is the best-smelling wood I know. It smells so great that people actually line chests and closets with it. And when the lovely bouquet begins to fade, you just give the wood a light sanding and reboot the aromatherapy.

The other outdoor wood you'll find at every home center is pressure-treated lumber. It also resists rot very well, and you can certainly build outdoor projects with it. It's a bit cheaper than cedar, and today's formulations are far less toxic than the old ones were. But pressure-treated wood is heavy and homely. It's not always called pressure-treated these days, but you'll recognize it either by its unnatural color (either from the chemicals or the stain manufacturers use to mimic other woods) or the pattern of dents on the surface that let the chemicals seep in during the treatment process. So I would use pressure-treated wood for large outdoor projects like fences and decks, but not when looks matter most.

There are other outdoor woods that are as beautiful as cedar, like redwood and ipé, but both are pricier and a little harder to find, and don't always come in the same array of sizes and shapes as cedar. Some other widely available outdoor woods also come from questionable sources, whereas almost all cedar is harvested sustainably these days. If that's important to you, look for FSC® (Forest Stewardship Council®) certification.

So cedar it is: Easy on tools, wallets, and backs; soft to the touch; and beautiful to the eye.

HOW TO BUY CEDAR

As with many weather-resistant woods, the heart of a cedar log is the most durable. The heartwood is the dark tan stuff that we all know and love. To cut costs, however, some suppliers sell cedar boards with cream-colored sapwood in them, from the outside of the log. That part of the wood lacks the chemicals that resist rot and will fall apart in just a couple of years outside.

WATCH OUT FOR THE WHITE. The creamier sapwood will rot much more quickly than the tan heartwood, so pick through the pile carefully and avoid boards like this one.

5

outdoor bench

So far in this book you've hacked a cabinet to make a rolling workstation, paused to party, and now you are ready to make real furniture from the ground up. Don't be scared: This Asian-inspired bench is elegantly simple, like all of my favorite projects.

The cool part of this bench is how the four pieces in each upright (or trestle) are screwed and glued together to create a perfect hole (called a mortise) for the beam to pass through. As for wood, you'll need one 2×6 and one 2×2, each 8 ft. long, and either a 10-ft. 2×4 or two 8-footers if that's all you can find. By the way, the parts are called 2×2s, 2×4s, etc., but they are actually ½ in. smaller than that in each dimension. You'll also need two boxes of deck screws, one 2½ in. long and the other 3 in. long.

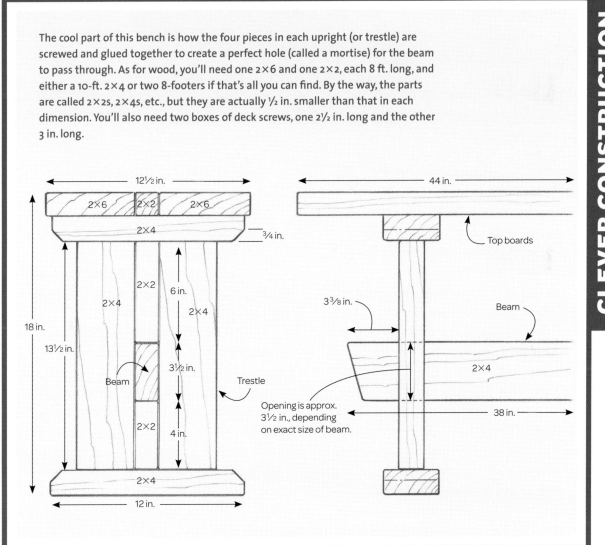

I first saw an outdoor bench like this one a long time ago, at the shop of a pro woodworker in Idaho, Mark Edmundson, who was selling them because they were so quick to make yet so pretty. Ten years later, when I set out to design a little bench for this book, made from standard deck boards and a box of screws, I didn't intend to copy Mark's design. But when I finished sketching and prototyping and refining, I realized I had come up with something similar, with the pieces of 2×2s and 2×4s in the uprights combining in a similar way to create the square hole for a long 2×4 beam to pass through. There just aren't that many ways to skin this cat, and Mark's method rules, apparently.

Luckily for me, and you, Edmundson didn't mind sharing his great idea (I checked!). Mark is a way better builder than me, and an accomplished author. Check out his book, *Pocket Hole Joinery* (The Taunton Press, 2014; www.taunton.com), which covers a simple but strong way to build sturdy cabinets and furniture of all sizes using a simple pocket hole jig.

This bench would be comfortable on a porch, patio, or deck, on grass or in a garden. It looks so good, I would even let it come indoors. Feel free to play with the size and design details of the bench. For example, you can make it as long as you want. But 18 in. tall will be about right for most body sizes.

For me what makes this bench Asian-inspired is the way the top overhangs the base and also how the beam sticks through the uprights and is beveled on its ends. The real beauty of this sturdy, stylish bench is that it is built with deck boards and deck screws (like cedar, these resist the weather). That's it. And you have to look hard to see any of the screws. By the way, you can apply an oil finish to darken the cedar and keep it tan for a bit longer, but ultimately it will weather to a silvery grey just the same. So I say don't bother with the oil.

TWO TYPES OF ANGLED CUTS

There are two ways you can move a miter saw for angled cuts, either tilting it over sideways or rotating it horizontally. It's easier to cut with it rotated than tilted, but do whatever makes sense for the cut you are making.

1 BEVEL THE FEET. The bottoms and tops of the uprights have small bevels on the end, which are pretty to look at and simple to cut on the miter saw. Start by marking a line 3/4 in. from the end to guide your cut. Then tilt the saw over to 45 degrees, line your mark up with the inside edge of the blade, and make the cut.

2 BEAM GETS ANGLED TOO. This time you'll need to pivot the saw table instead of tilting the saw. Mark the overall length of the beam, pivot the saw to 15 degrees, and cut at your mark. Simple. You're gonna love that miter saw.

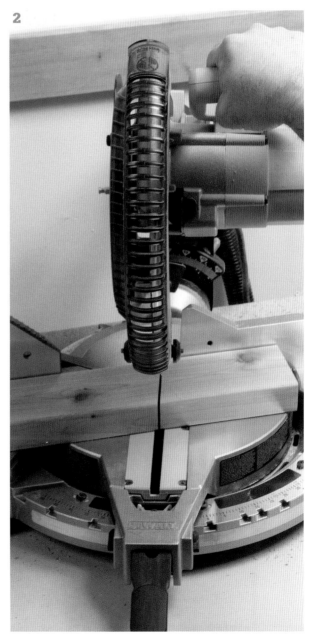

START WITH THE UPRIGHTS

By screwing and gluing four pieces together in the following sequence, you'll create a perfect hole for the long beam to pass through and a pair of strong uprights to support all butts large and small.

1 CUT AND MATCH THE PIECES. To create an accurate hole (mortise) for the 2×4 beam to pass through, the thickness of the 2×2's needs to match the 2×4 beam. The 2×2 probably isn't the same thickness in both directions, so after you cut all the pieces to length for the uprights, flip the 2×2 pieces each way to find the thickness that matches the thickness of the 2×4 most closely. **2 MARK THE SURFACES TO BE GLUED.** Check marks are an easy way to keep track of important surfaces on workpieces. **3 PREDRILL.** The small center pieces need clearance holes for the screws. Drill two holes in each piece. Don't go too close to the ends or you might split the pieces you are screwing into.

YELLOW GLUE BASICS

Cheap and available everywhere, yellow wood glue creates a powerful bond. In general, Titebond III® is your best bet. It gives you more working time than other versions (before it starts to seize up), and it also happens to be rated for both indoor and outdoor use, which is great for this bench project.

SAND AND SPREAD. Yellow glue likes flat, sanded surfaces, and to be spread out evenly with some kind of brush. If you do that, and clamp the pieces together tightly, the bond will be stronger than the wood itself.

4 SHORT PIECES FIRST. Feel with your fingertips to be sure the ends of the pieces are even as you screw them on. You don't need pilot holes in the lower pieces, as cedar is spongy and won't split easily. Use the longer screws here.   **5 NOW USE THE 2×4 AS A SPACER.** Take a cutoff piece of the same 2×4 used for the beam and use it to space the next piece you are attaching. Press that second 2×2 piece firmly against the 2×4 as you screw it on. Use glue and the long screws as before.   **6 THE LAST PIECE GETS CLAMPED ON.** Take away the 2×4 spacer block, spread glue on the two short pieces, and clamp on the last section of 2×4, making sure it is even with the end of the shorter middle piece. Try to keep the parts as flat as possible as you clamp them. If they are bowing one way or the other, it might help to put one of the two clamps on the opposite side.   **7 TRIM THE FAR END.** One end of the whole assembly should line up at this point, but the other ends of the pieces probably won't. You can trim them on the miter saw. Trim as much as you can with one thin slice, and if the saw can't quite reach the end, as shown here, flip the workpiece over, line up the blade with the trimmed edge, and nip off that last bit.

ADD THE TOP AND BOTTOM OF THE TRESTLES

1 MARK AND DRILL CLEARANCE HOLES.
Mark a centerline and then lay the feet
flat against the upright assembly to
mark the best locations for screws—not
too close to the edges of the pieces, to
prevent splitting. Then drill clearance
holes for the screws. **2 USE A SPACER
TO LINE UP THE PARTS DURING ASSEMBLY.**
The top and bottom pieces should be
centered on the center section. Place a
1-in.-thick spacer of some kind below
the uprights to line them up while you
drive in 3-in.-long screws. **3 BREAK
ALL THE EDGES.** Cut the rest of your
parts and pieces to size and then clean
up the corners. Workpieces look much
better if the sharp edges and splinters
are replaced by nice little bevels or
roundovers. A sanding block makes this
easy. **4 DRILL THROUGH THE TOPS OF
THE TRESTLES.** This is where you will
drive screws to attach the top boards
of the bench. The upright boards in the
trestle are similar to the top boards, so
use those as a visual guide for lining up
the screw holes. It's fine to drill at a slight
angle here.

5 INSERT THE BEAM. If you've lined up all the parts pretty well, the beam should slide in. Check the drawing on p. 63 to see how far it should stick out at both ends. **6 MAKE SURE EVERYTHING IS SQUARE.** Use your combo square to make sure the trestles are square to the beam in every direction.

7 DRILL AND DRIVE. Drill clearance holes on the inside corners of the beam, at a sharp angle so the screws will pass into the trestle. Do one hole on each side. Then drive in 3-in.-long screws, burying the heads so the screws are tight. That's all the grip you need on the beam. **8 ATTACH THE TOP BOARDS AND YOU'RE DONE.** Line them up and measure to be sure the base is located in the center. The two outside boards get two screws each, and the center strip gets one. Use 2½-in. screws here so they don't pop out the top. (I traded the cordless drill for a stubby screwdriver in the tight space under the beam.) Then sand the corners of the top boards and put the bench where everyone can see it.

PREP THE PARTS

This project is all square cuts, with the side boards getting a quick roundover on each corner from your sanding block, so this stage goes fast.

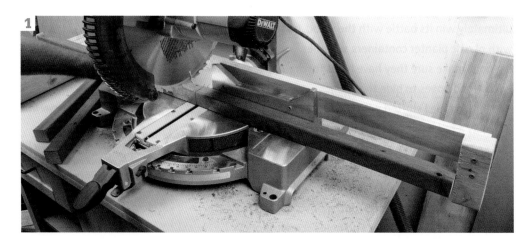

1 CHOP ALL OF THE PARTS TO LENGTH. Cut the posts to length, and then the side boards. (See the sidebar on the facing page for how to set up the stop shown here.) When cutting the side boards, note that you need an equal number of slightly longer and shorter ones. Also, make sure your planting container will fit, or adjust the lengths of the side boards. **2 AN EASY WAY TO ROUND THE CORNERS.** You want a roughly 1/4-in. to 3/8-in. roundover on the corners of the long side boards. To do that quickly and easily, use your sanding block and 80-grit paper to make a big bevel on the corner. Shoot for about 1/4 in. wide, but just trust your eyes. Then just sand the points at the ends of the bevel to create a smooth roundover.   **3 FINISH BY BREAKING THE EDGES.** Sand the ends and roundovers lightly to remove any whiskers and soften the edges.

USE A STOP FOR REPEAT CUTS

On any stationary power tool, like the miter saw, you can set up a stop when you need to cut a lot of pieces to the same length. It's a great timesaver that adds accuracy, too.

1 MEASURE JUST ONCE. After making a clean, square cut on the end of the board, mark the length you need. Then align that mark with the blade of the saw and keep the board right where it is.

2 SET UP A STOP. Screw a block to the end of a long thin board to create the type of work stop seen here, and then attach the stop to the fence of the miter saw. Most fences have holes for screwing on a stop as shown. If not, you can use clamps to attach the stop.

3 NOW CUT A PILE OF MATCHING PIECES. Just bump the board up against the stop and cut with no measuring. In a minute you'll have a pile of perfect pieces. Note: To hold down a workpiece on the right side of the saw, it's safer to switch hands than cross your arms.

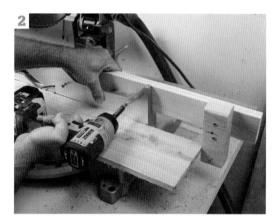

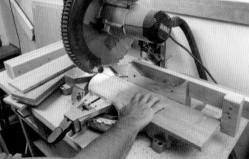

ATTACH THE SHORT BOARDS FIRST

To assemble the planter box, start by making two opposite sides, which are identical. The short boards should end right at the outside edges of the posts to set the overall width of the planter box, so attach those first as shown. Be sure to drill clearance and pilot holes (see p. 29) to give the screws their best grip and avoid splitting the wood.

1 DRILL CLEARANCE AND PILOT HOLES AS USUAL. Roughly locate the board to see where to drill clearance holes in it without drilling into the posts. Then place it precisely, with the ends even with the sides of the post and the top edges flush also, and drill smaller pilot holes into the post below. If your smaller drill bit won't reach far enough to do a full-depth hole, just dimple the post, take the board away, and finish the job.   **2 SCREW IT DOWN SOLIDLY.** Making sure the edges of the board are still aligned, drive 2-in.-long deck screws through the boards and into the posts.   **3 ATTACH THE SECOND SHORT BOARD.** Using one of the longer boards as a spacer, but without screwing it down, align the next short board with the outside of the posts, drill your clearance and pilot holes, and screw it down to lock the posts in the right position.

LONG BOARDS NEXT

These go on the same way, except you have to be sure to even out the overhang at each end. The last board will not quite cover the bottom ends of the posts, which are intended to stick out a bit at the bottom of the planter box.

1 CLEARANCE HOLES FIRST. Again, locate the boards roughly to see where to drill the clearance holes, but raise the boards a little so you don't drill into the posts below. **2 EVEN OUT THE OVERHANG.** Use your combination square to make sure each end sticks out the same amount, roughly 3/8 in., and then drill your pilot holes and drive screws.

NOW CONNECT THE SIDES

With two sides done, you can attach the rest of the boards and complete the box. Be sure to even out the overhang of the extra-long boards and butt the ends of the short boards tightly against their neighbors when attaching them.

1 WEAVE IN THE OTHER BOARDS. Flip over the two sides you already assembled so they are standing on their top ends. Notice how the feet stick out a bit. Then weave in the remaining boards to hold everything in place temporarily.
2 BOTTOM BOARD FIRST. Screw on the bottom board to hold the box together. Mark the hole locations, making sure they will clear the screws in the board on the adjacent side. Then drill clearance holes, put the board back in place with its ends tight, drill pilot holes, and drive screws. **3 WORK YOUR WAY DOWN.** Now you can attach the rest of the boards, one by one. On the long boards, mark clearance holes, drill them, and even out the overhang before drilling pilot holes. **4 SCREW ON THE REST OF THE BOARDS.** Drive screws to attach this board, then follow the same steps to attach the ones below. **5 FLIP THE BOX TO FINISH THE JOB.** You can lay the box on its side to attach the remaining boards—the same way as all the others.

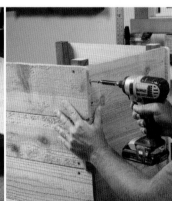

HOW TO TURN TWO PLANTERS INTO A BENCH

It's easy to attach a few seat boards and turn your planters into a little oasis.

1 CUT A COUPLE OF CLEATS. Use some leftover post material to make two cleats. Bevel their ends so they won't show as much under the seat. **2 DRILL CLEARANCE HOLES.** Place these holes about 1 in. from the ends and roughly ¼ in. to ⅜ in. from the top edge. **3 DRILL PILOT HOLES.** The cleat is aligned with the top edge of the third board and centered side to side. Use the clearance holes to align the pilot holes, drilling as far as the small bit will allow. Then remove the cleat to finish the pilot holes. If they don't miss the screws used to attach the side board, you can pull those screws. The cleat screws will do the same job.

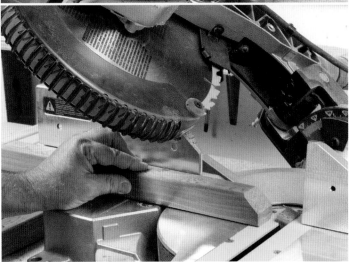

4

5

4 ONE LAST HOLE. This one is a clearance hole so you can drive a screw into the cleat from inside the box. **5 ATTACH THE CLEATS.** Use 3-in.-long screws to attach the cleats, then drive shorter screws (1⅝ in. if you have them) from the inside to add additional strength. Be sure to drill pilot holes first. **6 CUT AND DRILL THE SEAT BOARDS.** After cutting the three boards to length (48 in. each), drill clearance holes for the screws that will attach them. Note the lines I drew to show where to drill so the screws would be centered on the cleats below. **7 DROP THEM IN.** Space the planter boxes the right distance apart and drop in the seat boards. **8 A FEW SCREWS MAKE THEM PERMANENT.** Drill pilot holes down into the cleats. The small bit won't reach far enough, so remove the seat boards to finish the job. Then screw them down permanently with 3-in.-long screws. **9 PLANTS NEED A BOOST.** The plastic pots were too short for these tall planter boxes, so I gave them a boost with a few old paint cans. Then the plants dropped in at the right level. You don't need to do this with the shorter version of the planter boxes.

7

6

8

9

CEDAR PLANTERS WITH AN OPTIONAL BENCH

5

build a cutting board and add some router skills

A CUTTING BOARD is a great project at any stage of your journey. You can make them as simple or as fancy as you want, in all sorts of shapes for different tasks. And they are small enough to make in batches as gifts.

Most cutting board designs combine strips of different woods into a sort of crazy quilt. But you'll need a tablesaw to create those strips. We are going to go the elegantly simple route again—taking a naturally beautiful piece of wood and bringing out its best. We'll do that with gleaming curves and your first real wood finish: a wipe-on oil that lets viewers see deep into the shimmering wood grain.

For this cutting board design you'll need to add a tool to your growing arsenal: a small router, sometimes called a trim router or laminate trimmer. Like your other power tools, the router will pay dividends for decades to come.

Let's start by finding the right piece of wood. You might find it in your bin of wood scraps. If you are just starting out as a woodie, ask around the lumberyard or at the hardwood dealer for "shorts" or "cutoffs" with nice "figure," which refers to the grain pattern. You can usually get these for cheap, and they make great cutting boards and small boxes. Ask for pieces that are already surfaced smooth, not roughsawn. That's what I did in this case, finding a piece of white oak with beautiful grain. I actually bought a whole board, planning to make a series of cutting boards from it.

A lot of people spend a lot of time talking about the safest woods and finishes for cutting boards, but it's really not that scary or complicated. Avoid woods known for causing allergic reactions. Rosewood, cocobolo, sassafras, yew, and olivewood are a few to watch out for, but those are rare anyway and almost any other hardwood is OK. Avoid softwoods like pine, alder, fir, and poplar, which won't stand up well to sharp knives.

The king of the cutting-board woods is maple. It is hard as heck, it has super-tight grain (tiny pores) so it is easy to wipe off and clean, and the grain often ripples into curly patterns that look amazing under a coat of oil. But almost any hardwood will do. Cutting boards are pretty simple in design, basically putting the wood on display, so look for a board that is special-looking on its own.

As for wood finishes, they are all fine. All finishes are nontoxic once dry, despite popular belief. That said, thin oil finishes are better than thick varnishes because oil can be renewed when it gets dull, whereas thick film finishes like polyurethane will just get scarred and flaky over time and have to be sanded off completely.

curvy cutting board

This simple cutting board uses just one short piece of wood, but it will teach you about curves, routers, and how to apply a gorgeous finish. It will also make you the envy of your guests.

GOOD WOODS FOR CUTTING BOARDS. The harder the wood, the better it will stand up to sharp knives. Be sure to get a board that has been planed smooth on both sides. This is white oak, with almost perfectly vertical grain (look at the end of the board). That creates cool stripes on the face of the board, called "ray fleck."

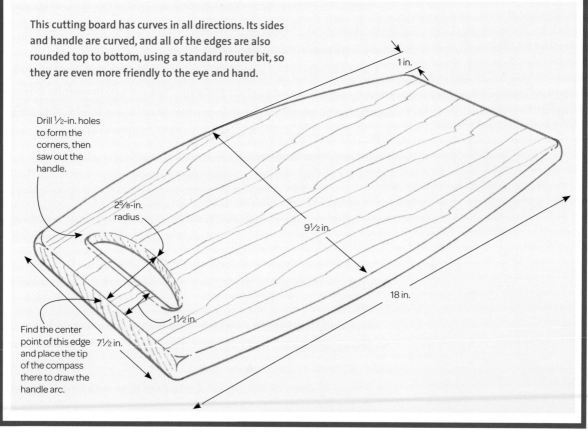

This cutting board has curves in all directions. Its sides and handle are curved, and all of the edges are also rounded top to bottom, using a standard router bit, so they are even more friendly to the eye and hand.

Drill ½-in. holes to form the corners, then saw out the handle.

2⅝-in. radius

1½ in.

1 in.

9½ in.

18 in.

Find the center point of this edge and place the tip of the compass there to draw the handle arc.

7½ in.

BUILD A CUTTING BOARD AND ADD SOME ROUTER SKILLS

LAY OUT THE CUTS

1 CUT TO LENGTH. If the board is too wide for your miter saw, use the circular-saw guide to get a straight, smooth cut at each end. Make sure the guide is square to the board and elevate both of them in order to clamp everything down so it doesn't move.   **2 BEND A STICK TO DRAW A CURVE.** Any consistently thin ruler or strip of wood or metal will do. Tap in a couple of nails at the ends of the curve, just inside the waste area. Then mark the center point of the curve and push the stick to that point to draw a beautiful arc.   **3 LAY OUT THE HANDLE.** Use your combo square to draw a line 1½ in. from one end. Then set a compass to 2⅝ in. and put the point near the outside edge, right at the center point, and mark the curved part of the handle.

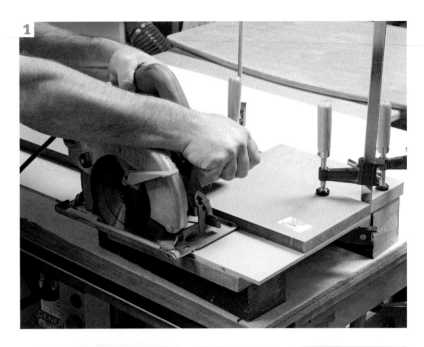

SAW OUT THE HANDLE

A jigsaw is perfect for this job. You just need a hole to get it started. In this case, we'll drill two, forming the round ends of the handle.

1 MARK THE HOLE LOCATIONS. Because these ½-in. holes will serve as the ends of the handle opening, we want to drill them in just the right spot. Measure across the ends of the opening to center the drill bit so it will just touch both lines. Mark that spot, and then dimple it with a nail. **2 DRILL IN STAGES.** This is a big hole, in a hard wood, so start with a small drill bit and work your way up to the full ½ in. Normal drill bits will follow each other, centering themselves in the smaller holes. However, if you have a ½-in. brad-point or Forstner bit you should do the hole in one shot. Notice the piece of waste wood below the cutting board. That will prevent splintering on the bottom of the holes. **3 SAW HOLE TO HOLE.** Start at the outside edge of the hole so there is no bump between the hole and the jigsaw cut. Saw along the inside edge of the lines, and try to cut smoothly into the outside edge of the opposite hole so you have less sanding to do later.

BUILD A CUTTING BOARD AND ADD SOME ROUTER SKILLS

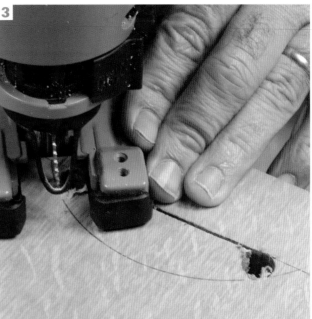

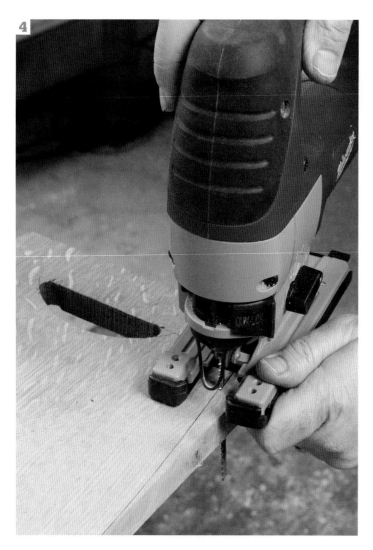

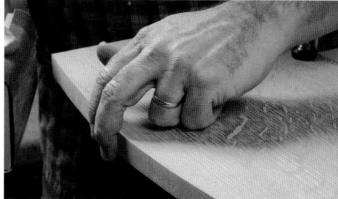

4 NOW CUT THE OUTSIDE CURVE. If your board is wider than the 9½ in. needed, you'll have more wood to rest on as you cut. In my case I used the whole width of my board, so I was careful to keep the jigsaw flat on the wood so the cut would be square.   **5 SAND THE OUTSIDE EDGES.** The round bearing on the router bit (see facing page) will follow any bumps, so you want to eliminate them now. Use your sanding block with rough 80-grit paper to smooth out your jigsaw cuts. To find bumps, feel with your fingers. They are an excellent guide. Do the straight ends of the board too.   **6 A SANDING TRICK FOR THE HANDLE.** Use some thick but flexible rubber to back your sandpaper. I use an old rubber mat, which makes the curves smoother and also fits inside small spaces. Note that I clamped the board in a nice vertical position here.

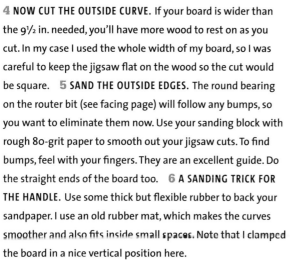

BUILD A CUTTING BOARD AND ADD SOME ROUTER SKILLS

ROUTER 101

A compact router like this DeWalt® 611 is a great one to start with. It's strong enough for most jobs yet very easy to control.

BEARING-GUIDED BITS. The bearing rides the edge, controlling the cut. This is a 3/8-in. roundover bit, but all sorts of shapes are available. Shanks come in 1/4-in.- and 1/2-in.-dia. sizes. Make sure you get the size that fits your router.

HOW TO INSERT A ROUTER BIT. Take off the router base if you can and push in the bit as far as it will go. Then, to be sure it will tighten properly, pull it out about 1/4 in. or so (top) before tightening the chuck, called a collet (above). Most of today's routers have a button that locks the spindle as you tighten the collet with a wrench. Others require two wrenches.

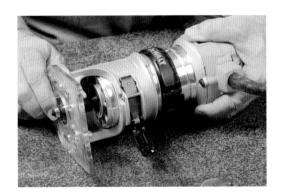

SLIDE ON THE BASE AND SET THE DEPTH. Read the manual to find out how to attach the base and adjust it up and down to change the depth of the router bit.

ROUTING THE EDGES

This is a good project for learning basic routing. Hold the router firmly as you turn it on, and make sure the bit is free and clear when you do. Then place the base on the wood and move the bit and bearing toward the edge you are working on. Now you can start routing that edge.

1 SET THE DEPTH FIRST. Mark a centerline and set the depth of the router bearing so at least its top edge touches the line. **2 CLAMP AND ROUT.** Clamp down the cutting board and rout in a counterclockwise direction around the board, against the rotation of the bit. That will make the router easy to control. Use one hand to hold the router and the other to keep its base flat on the wood. Start in the middle of an edge, not at a corner, and then feel the bearing on the router bit wrap around each corner as you go from edge to edge. You'll need to reposition the board and clamps to complete the job.

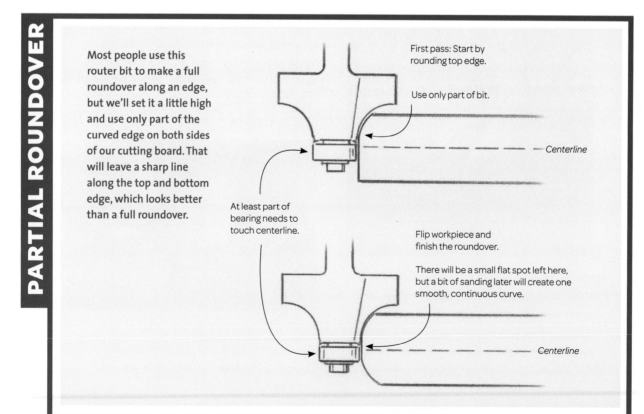

PARTIAL ROUNDOVER

Most people use this router bit to make a full roundover along an edge, but we'll set it a little high and use only part of the curved edge on both sides of our cutting board. That will leave a sharp line along the top and bottom edge, which looks better than a full roundover.

At least part of bearing needs to touch centerline.

First pass: Start by rounding top edge.

Use only part of bit.

Centerline

Flip workpiece and finish the roundover.

There will be a small flat spot left here, but a bit of sanding later will create one smooth, continuous curve.

Centerline

BUILD A CUTTING BOARD AND ADD SOME ROUTER SKILLS

3 ROUT INSIDE THE HANDLE, TOO. This time, move clockwise around the shape. Keep the router moving steadily to avoid burn marks and make an extra pass to remove any bumps from the first one.

4 NOW THE FLIP SIDE. After moving your clamps to rout all of the edges on one side, flip over the cutting board to rout the edges on the opposite side. Notice that there is just enough of a flat spot left on the edge for the bearing to ride on. Use your sanding tools to turn the router cuts and that little flat into one smooth curve along the edges and inside the handle area.

5 ADD FEET IF YOU LIKE. I found these non-skid plastic feet at my local home center. They'll raise the board off the countertop so it dries more easily after being rinsed off.

HOW TO APPLY A BEAUTIFUL OIL FINISH

A beautiful finish is all about preparation. If you sand the right way, you'll get an amazing finish on any wood. Be sure to back up your paper with a block for all the flat surfaces.

1 WORK THROUGH THE GRITS. When sanding the edges and faces of this cutting board, or any project, work progressively from rougher grits like 120-grit up through the finer grits: 150-grit, 220-grit, and 320-grit. Each successive grit makes finer scratches, removing the rough scratches from the previous one, ending with scratches so fine they will just look like a smooth sheen under an oil finish. **2 VACUUM AWAY THE DUST.** This is the best way to get sanding dust out of the pores in the wood so the grain looks its best. Compressed air also works, or a wipe with a T-shirt if nothing else. **3 THE MAGIC MOMENT.** When you wipe on that first coat of oil finish, you finally see the grain in all its glory. Buy any clear (not tinted or colored) oil finish designed for wiping and you should be fine. Don't stain the wood! Nice woods are beautiful on their own, and a great stain or dye job is difficult to pull off successfully.

4 WIPE ON, WIPE OFF. Wait 5 or 10 minutes after wiping on a generous coat of oil, and then buff it off with clean cloth or paper towels. By the way, disposable vinyl gloves are awesome for finishing, saving you a lot of hand-washing.　**5 SAND BETWEEN COATS.** Wait at least 6 hours and then sand lightly with 320-grit. You don't need a block this time. Just fold over the paper and sand lightly to smooth away the little dust nibs and wood whiskers that tend to rise after the first coat.　**6 JUST TWO COATS FOR A CUTTING BOARD.** Apply one more coat of oil, wiping it on and buffing it off. Let it dry for 24 hours, and then enjoy the buttery smoothness of your first real wood finish.

6

plumbing pipe plus plywood equals high fashion

IF YOU WALK INTO a home center with your creative hat on (I picture it as something Swiss, with a giant feather), you'll find all sorts of things to build with. Plumbing pipes are a great example.

I first used this system of threaded pipes and connectors with a couple of kidney-shaped pieces of plywood to create a built-in desk and shelf system for my young daughter. Go online and you'll find tons of DIY projects using this screw-together building system, from lighting to kitchen islands to furniture of all kinds.

The industrial look isn't for everyone, but I love it, and I love building with it. The bins of fittings and flanges are the adult version of the Tinkertoy® set I had as a kid—just as fun and versatile, but much stronger and more durable. The pipe comes in a plain black steel finish and a silvery grey galvanized coating, so you have some design options.

For connecting to tabletops, walls, or floors, the wide flanges are the key component. They thread onto the end of the pipe and have holes for screwing and bolting through.

This project combines these pipes and fittings with some nice birch plywood you might not know about. Called Baltic or Russian birch, it has many thin, stripey layers that show at the edges. People often cover the edges of plywood with strips of solid wood when building furniture or cabinets, but these cool edges—when polished and finished—fit right in with the industrial chic of the plumbing pipe.

You can get this better grade of plywood at high-end lumberyards and hardwood retailers. Just call ahead and they'll tell you if they have it. They can even chop it down for you to a more manageable size, so you can get it home easier. For the tables in this chapter, you could have it cut into 2-ft. by 4-ft. pieces, which would fit in a Smart car.

For these living-room designs I went with the galvanized pipe. It has a more refined look than the black pipe, and ties in better with the light-colored plywood. You'll notice I said designs, plural. I knew I wanted to do a coffee table with a low shelf underneath, but when I was trying out all sorts of shapes for the shelf and tabletop, I found two approaches that I loved equally. So I built both. Choose whatever you like, or come up with a shape of your own.

DESIGN 101

You'll learn two super-valuable lessons in this project. One is applying a protective polyurethane finish. The other is designing using prototypes.

A lot of people blow right through the design stage to get to the building part, diving in with just a rough sketch or a rough idea. That can be fun and freeing, but it can also lead to disappointment. You usually either end up trashing your project midstream—a big waste of time and materials—or fight through to the end and then live with a project you aren't really happy with.

It's a shame because the design stage can be fun, and there are lots of ways to tackle it. Whereas some folks use computer programs to dial in every detail, I find those a little tedious and sometimes misleading. For me and many others, there is nothing like seeing your design in the real world. That's why I generally use sketches and prototypes. The sketches are pretty rough, mostly for brainstorming, and just detailed enough to get me to the prototype stage.

A prototype is a full-size model of your project, or some key part of it, made from whatever cheap material is easiest. My favorite cheap material for prototypes is rigid foam insulation, available in 3/4-in.- and 1 1/2-in.-thick panels. I used the thinner stuff here to simulate the thickness of the plywood (see "Make Cheap Prototypes for a True Preview" on the facing page). I did the same for the cutting board in the last chapter.

You can zip through the foam panels with normal woodworking tools, so it only takes a few minutes to try something out. And you can use tape or whatever to attach panels and pieces to each other.

a more protective finish

On high-wear surfaces like a tabletop, it's nice to have a more durable finish than the thin wipe-on oil we used on the cutting board. So the other great lesson here is how to apply a thicker, more lustrous wood finish that also offers more protection.

I'll be brushing on Minwax®'s fast-drying oil-based polyurethane to create a tough tabletop finish that you can use on almost any project. Like the wiped-on finish, this one also has oil that brings out the deep shimmering patterns in the wood grain, but the film you build up acts like a lens, only deepening the luster.

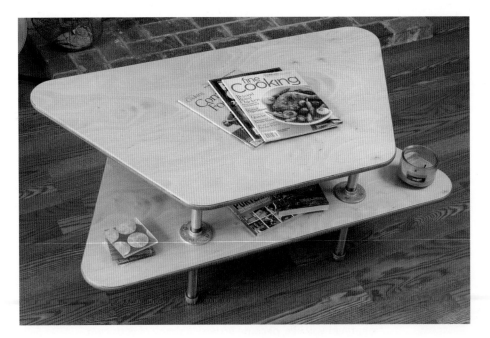

TWO DESIGNS. In the first design (see p. 92), the boat-shaped top and shelf echo each other. In the other (shown here), the shapes are still identical, but one is flipped to create interesting wings above and below. Because each part is only 24 in. wide, you can get all four from one 8-ft.-long sheet of plywood.

MAKE CHEAP PROTOTYPES FOR A TRUE PREVIEW

You can draw all you want, but nothing shows what a project will really look like better than a full-size prototype. I often use ¾-in.-thick foam insulation to mimic wood. It's cheap and easy to cut and shape.

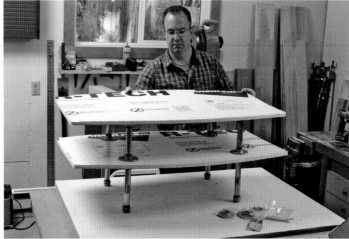

TABLE DESIGNS WERE A TIE. I was able to attach the bolts right through the stiff foamboard, letting me try out a few different shapes. I even tried the designs out in my living room.

BORING BOARDS. I rejected a number of cutting boards before dialing in the right shape for the board and the handle.

8 postmodern coffee table(s)

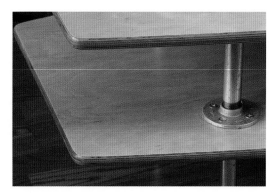

Cut your high-end plywood into any shapes you want, add plumbing fixtures from your local home center, and you can make a coffee table fit for the hippest Brooklyn loft.

NICE COMBO. Baltic-birch plywood has stripey layers at the edges, which look great when polished and finished. The industrial look works well with the plumbing hardware.

BASIC ANATOMY

Coffee tables have a standard height, around 18 in., which works well for people seated in sofas. So use the following pipe sizes, but feel free to design your own tabletop and shelf shapes.

Tabletop

All pipe and pipe hardware is ¾-in. size, with galvanized finish.

6-in. pipe

#10, ¾-in.-long flat-head wood screws hold the top on.

¾-in. pipe flanges

Shelf

Approx. 18 in.

8-in. pipe

¼-in.-dia., 1½-in.-long flat-head bolts pass through the shelf, with washers and nuts on bottom side.

¾-in. pipe caps

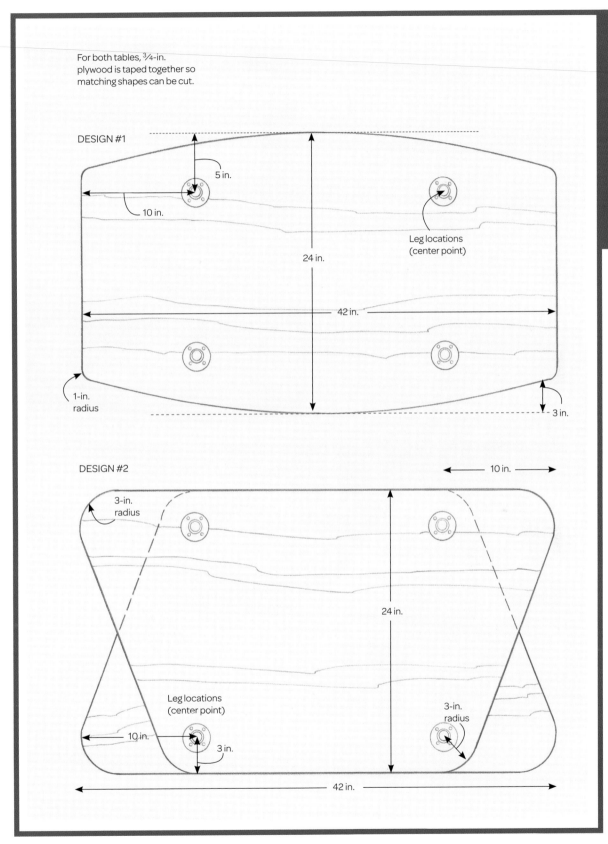

For both tables, ¾-in. plywood is taped together so matching shapes can be cut.

DESIGN #1

5 in.

10 in.

Leg locations
(center point)

24 in.

42 in.

1-in.
radius

3 in.

DESIGN #2

10 in.

3-in.
radius

24 in.

Leg locations
(center point)

3-in.
radius

10 in.

3 in.

42 in.

PREPARE THE PARTS

There are two different designs to choose from, and either can come from one 4-ft. by 4-ft. piece of Baltic-birch plywood. You'll probably have to buy a full 4×8 sheet, so just save the rest for another project.

1 CHOP UP YOUR PLYWOOD. The good folks at your home center or lumberyard can use their panel saw to cut the big 4×8 sheets in half or smaller for easier transport. At home, use your saw guide to cut the parts to final overall size. Make sure they all come out the same size. **2 LAYOUT FIRST.** For the trapezoid shapes (Design #2 on p. 97), start by marking the centers of the circular corners and then use a compass to draw the arcs you need. Then connect the arcs with straight lines. For the boat-shaped design (Design #1), use the trick from the cutting board project to draw the curves. A long aluminum ruler works nicely for this long curve.

PLUMBING PIPE PLUS PLYWOOD EQUALS HIGH FASHION

STACK PARTS FOR SPEED AND ACCURACY

By stacking the two parts, you can cut and smooth both at the same time, which is faster and guarantees a perfect match.

1 THE SECRET IS DOUBLE-FACED TAPE. Get the thicker type that has a thin web of fabric in it. Be sure to stick it inside the edges of your layout.

2 HOW TO LINE UP THE PARTS. Put a stick of wood at the far side to keep the tape from sticking while you line up the corners closest to you. Then reach across, pull out the stick, and let the top sheet drop. Bang your fist over the taped areas for a strong bond.   **3 SAW THE STRAIGHT LINES.** Use your circular saw and saw guide to cut the long angled sides of the trapezoids, connecting the arcs drawn at the corners.

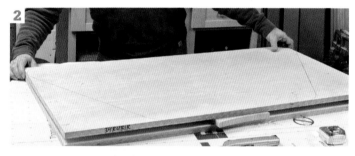

4 JIGSAW THE CURVES. Use the jigsaw to cut the long curves on one table or the tight ones on the other. To keep the saw from tipping and making an angled cut, hold the inside edge of the base flat on the plywood.

5 LOTS OF SANDING. Use your sanding block to smooth the curves, using 80-grit paper.

6 HOW TO GET THE PARTS APART. Double-faced tape can have a very strong grip. To pry the parts apart without damaging them, a wide palette knife works well. Tap it between the parts, and then pry steadily and let the tape slowly release, one area at a time.

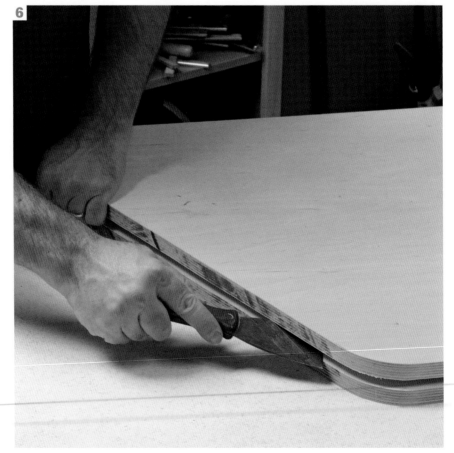

ROUT THE EDGES

These edges have the same shape as the edges of the cutting board.

1 START WITH THE CENTERLINES. As before, mark the centerline of the edge and then set the depth so at least the top part of the bearing will touch that line. **2 ROUT, FLIP, AND ROUT.** Just as on the cutting board, rout one side first, repositioning and reclamping the workpiece as needed, before flipping it over and doing the same on the other side.

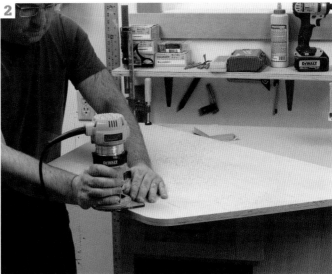

As before, we'll use just part of the ³⁄₈-in.-radius bit on both sides of the edge, leaving just enough of a flat spot in the middle for the router bearing to ride on. A bit of sanding afterward will turn this edge into one smooth curve.

PARTIAL ROUNDOVER

PAUSE FOR LAYOUT AND DRILLING

Bolts pass through the shelf to connect the pipe flanges above and below it. Before final sanding, lay out and drill the holes in the shelf for the bolts. Check the drawings for pipe and flange locations. Do not drill the top panel yet!

1 USE A PIPE FLANGE AS A DRILL GUIDE. After marking the center of each hole, center the flange on the mark by eye and then mark circles inside the bolt holes.
2 DRILL THE SHELF. Start by tapping a nail in the center of each of the circles you drew, and then drill through the shelf with a ¼-in. drill bit.   **3 SAND THE EDGES SMOOTH.** I used a piece of a thick rubber mat to back my sandpaper as I turned the routed edges on the top and shelf into one smooth curve. Start with 120-grit and work your way through 150-grit and then 220-grit.

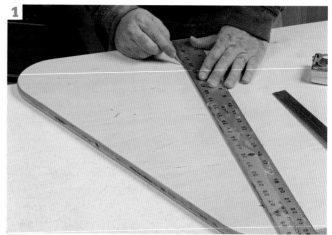

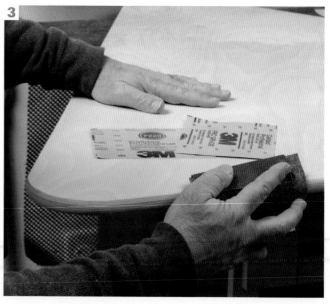

PLUMBING PIPE PLUS PLYWOOD EQUALS HIGH FASHION

RANDOM-ORBIT SANDER TAMES BIG SURFACES

You can smooth the big flat faces of the plywood with your sanding block, but this might be a good time to invest in a random-orbit sander. At just $50 to $60, the 5-in.-dia. size is your best value.

HOOK-AND-LOOP DISCS. These Velcro®-like discs go on and off easily. Be sure to line up the holes in the disk and sander for effective dust collection.

ALWAYS CONNECT THE SANDER TO A SHOP VACUUM. Removing the dust keeps it out of your lungs, and also makes the sandpaper last longer.

SLOW AND STEADY. Don't press down hard, and don't move the sander back and forth quickly like a sanding block (it's already vibrating back and forth!). Just keep it flat, and move it in a steady pattern that you can keep track of so you sand the whole surface evenly. Don't over sand any one area of plywood or you could sand through the veneer and reveal the dark glueline beneath.

FINISHING WITH OIL-BASED POLYURETHANE

Oil-based poly is a thick durable finish for high-wear items like tables. As with any finish, good surface preparation makes all the difference. That's why we sanded so carefully.

FAST-DRYING SATIN. With a fast-drying polyurethane in a warm workspace, you can sand it and add another coat within a few hours. Choose the satin sheen for a soft glow on furniture. Warning: Satin finishes have solids that settle to the bottom. That gunk needs to be stirred for a while until it blends back into the finish. Stir it occasionally when using it too.

1 START ON THE FLATS. Elevate the workpiece on some boards so you can access the edges. Foam brushes are disposable and work well for polyurethane. Unload the brush on the flat surfaces, staying away from the edges at first to avoid drips. Then make passes that start in the middle and go off the edges to smooth and finish off the surface with minimal dripping.   **2 EDGES LAST.** Without dipping the brush in the finish again, work it around the curved edges, to wet them without causing drips.   **3 CHECK FOR DRIPS AND LET IT DRY.** Run a paper towel along the bottom edge to smooth any drips. Then wait 4 to 6 hours for the finish to harden before flipping over the workpiece and doing the same on the other side. You'll be hitting the edges twice but that's no problem.   **4 SAND LIGHTLY AND VACUUM.** Let the finish dry for 12 hours, and then use 220-grit sandpaper to smooth the now-rough surfaces. Use your sanding block on the flat parts and your rubber backer on the curved edges. Sand just enough for a smooth feel, and then vacuum or wipe away the dust.   **5 RE-COAT AND REPEAT.** Put another coat on each side, and wait another day before sanding again, even more lightly this time, holding the sandpaper in your hand.

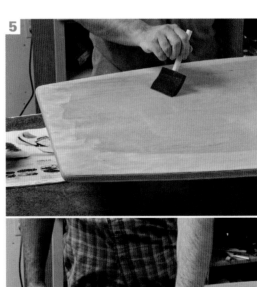

6 SANDPAPER TRICK. To fold a piece of sandpaper so no rough edges hit and dull each other, start by creasing it in both directions, and tearing one seam to the middle. Then fold it as shown. Unfold and refold it to expose the unused faces. **7 WIPE HARD AND RE-COAT.** Polyurethane dust can be a bit rubbery and needs a good wipe to be removed. Put on one last coat of finish (careful this time), and you should be done. But wait another day or so to attach the hardware.

PUT IT ALL TOGETHER

1 PREP THE PIPES. Attach all your feet and flanges, screwing everything on tight, and use a stick to make sure all of the parts are the same height. Wipe off any grease or price-tag gunk with paint thinner.

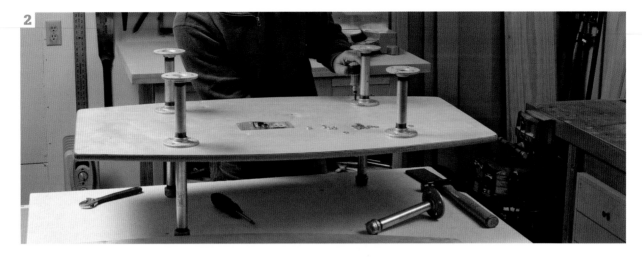

2 NUTS AND BOLTS. Flat-head bolts go through the top flanges and pass right down through the ones below the shelf. Then nuts and washers go on to hold everything together tightly. **3 ATTACH THE TOP.** Position the top under the whole assembly, bottom side up, and use your combo square to be sure the edges of the top and shelf are aligned. Then use the holes in the flanges under the tabletop to mark the locations of the pilot holes you need. Now drill small pilot holes at those locations and screw on the top. Be careful how deep you drill! **4 FLAG TRICK.** To avoid drilling through the top of the table, measure how deep you want to drill and attach a little tape flag at that point. When the tape wipes away the chips, you know it's time to stop drilling.

7

add-on legs
make tables easy

IN THE LAST CHAPTER, we used plumbing pipe hardware to create two coffee tables. That system works great for connecting things, but the pipes are a little skinny to use as legs on their own, especially if the table is taller than knee height. Also, the industrial look isn't suited to every project or everyone's taste. Lucky for us there are other awesomely easy ways to add legs to any slab of wood and create tables and desks of all sizes. In this chapter we'll check out three of them.

Along the way you'll learn how to find and use a big live-edge wood slab, which will draw the most oohs and ahhs of anything you build. Trust me on that. And as a bonus I'll take a shallow dive into one of the best furniture styles of the past 100 years: Mid-Century Modern. Let's start there.

WHY DESIGN HISTORY MATTERS

If you bought this book you have a strong desire to do things yourself, from remodeling your apartment, house, or condo to crafting handmade projects big and small. So it's worth a short trip back into the history of design. If you ignore it, you'll be blending elements that don't really mesh, and wondering why you don't love the look of what you're building.

You already know a lot of design history. It starts with where you grew up, and the houses and furnishings you saw around you. And then there is every place you've visited and enjoyed, and every movie and TV show you've seen. If you are from New England, you might like the old Colonial houses and furniture that are all around you. Or you might hate them, thinking of that old boring stuff as mom's house. If you grew up out West, you might feel the same love or loathing for the Mission style.

You might not know what these styles are called, but I guarantee you already have strong feelings about what you like when you see it.

If you want to build things that look really great, it's worth learning what those basic historical styles are. That way you'll know why Greek columns look weird on a Colonial-style house. Or why fancy moldings look cool on period furniture or in a Renaissance cathedral but out of place on an Arts and Crafts cabinet.

mid-century modern style

Today the trends come and go quickly, and styles are all over the place. Most would agree that the last major identifiable design era ended about 50 years ago. It also happens to be one of my faves. If you look at the furniture and interiors in the TV show *Mad Men,* you'll get the picture. It's called Mid-Century Modern, and Danish Modern is a close cousin.

These Mid-Century styles are all about clean lines and natural materials, and they blend well with Asian influences and organic details like the live edge on the slab we'll use in this chapter. Mid-Century Modern also often combines metal, plastic, wood, and concrete, so anything goes, materialswise. Best of all, it looks awesome in today's houses and apartments.

Google the Bauhaus movement in Europe, and then Mid-Century Modern, which was the American offshoot. Try not to be inspired as heck. I dare you.

ADD-ON LEGS MAKE TABLES EASY

A VERSATILE STYLE

As this chapter shows, you don't have to be a furniture master to make projects in the clean, modern Mid-Century style. But just for fun, here are three masterful pieces from great furniture makers, to show you what's possible.

CLEAN CURVES. Mario Rodriguez's coffee table is inspired by Danish Modern design, with clean modern lines that put the beautiful mahogany on display.

MODERN MEETS RUSTIC. Jon Sterling built this bench from a live-edge slab and added Mid-Century legs, much like we'll do in this chapter.

SCANDINAVIA MEETS ASIA. Mark Edmundson's bench mixes Asian legs with a Swedish Mid-Century design and a seat woven from Danish cord.

slab madness

Wood slabs are awesome. They take a bit more work to find and flatten than normal boards, but I'll show you how to overcome those obstacles and enter the woodworking promised land. Of all the things you'll ever build, none will have the wow factor of your slab pieces. There is something about the scale, the curvy edges, and the beautiful grain and natural "defects" that makes you feel like you brought the soul of a living tree into your home. Check out the marvelous transformation our slab goes through and you'll see just what I mean.

where to find slabs and what to look for

To find big slabs like this one, you'll need to do a bit of minor digging. I got mine by asking around my local woodworking club, whose kind members suggested a local pro who might have some extra slabs on hand. Sure enough, Alexander Anderson had one for me at his shop in Northeast Portland. It was $250, which might seem steep, but not when you see the end result, which will make me happy for a lifetime.

A Google search and a few phone calls will also locate local hardwood dealers that specialize in slabs. You'll pay a bit more for their slabs, but they'll also have a bigger selection than most private individuals.

When choosing a wood slab, aside from finding the size and thickness that suits the purpose or space at hand, the main criterion is that the slab has been dried properly and thoroughly. That either means it was dried slowly in a kiln, or stacked outdoors and left to air-dry slowly until all of its water had evaporated from deep within. Speaking of indoors, look for slabs that have been stored there for a while. If yours is still sitting outdoors, it could still have a ways to go to come down to the same level as the drier indoor air.

If a slab is severely warped, it was probably brought indoors too early or kiln-dried too fast. So

the "build stuff" take on this sleek style

I always intended to make one project in this book from a live-edge wood slab with bolt-on legs. But when I dug into the legs available online, the possibilities multiplied. My two favorites are both in the Mid-Century style, which makes a beautiful marriage with live-edge slabs. So I went with both of them.

The three-rod hairpin legs are a Mid-Century classic. I got mine from www.rockler.com, a peerless purveyor of all things woodworking, and especially kind to newbies. They are dining-table height, so I attached them to our walnut slab and made a small desk (see the photo on p. 110).

The tapered walnut round legs are another Mid-Century option, this time from www.tablelegs.com. They screw into a walnut bracket, which in turn screws to the bottom of your walnut slab (see the photo above). Couldn't be easier.

As for the term *live-edge slab,* "live edge" means the sawmill left the original bark edge on at least one side of a big board, and "slab" means that board is big and thick and wide, suitable for a tabletop or bench seat all on its own (vs. gluing together narrower boards).

bring along a straightedge of some kind, like your long aluminum ruler. If the slab is warped by more than ¼ in., don't buy it—unless you are comfortable with losing a lot of its thickness when flattening it.

Three other things to avoid are unstable knots, long cracks, and rotted wood. Knots are fine as long as they aren't going to fall out, leaving big chunks missing. Short cracks are okay too, but long ones will make the whole slab unstable. To find rotted wood, look for insect holes and also discolored, crumbly areas.

In the walnut slab I bought there were some cracks at the ends from the drying process, but there was enough extra length so I could just cut those sections off. I cut off most of a big knot too, but left some of it in my finished top. Perfectly imperfect.

Aside from hiring a pro to flatten the slab (see the sidebar below), you can do everything else yourself, as you'll see in this chapter, making you a slab master until the end of time, able to turn out glowing examples of nature's splendor. Now you'll have some real skills to go along with that beard, tattoo, or other totem of badassedness. (I can't pull off any of those accoutrements, so I just keep it clean and simple, like Mid-Century Modern does.)

HIRE A PRO TO FLATTEN YOUR SLAB

Slabs are wide and often have defects like cracks and knots, and even the best ones will have curved and warped a bit as they dried. Even if you had a jointer and planer—two big milling machines for wood—the slab would be too wide for them. Hand tools will flatten them, but it's a tricky process that's outside the scope of this book. So you'll need to buy some time at an industrial woodworking shop with a big wide-belt sander. Again, local pro woodworkers or club members might be able to point you in the right direction.

I found a millwork shop in Portland that would flatten my slab for around $50. I cut off some of the waste to make it shorter, threw it in my truck, and just

CALL IN A PRO. If you bring your slab to a professional millwork shop, they'll flatten and smooth it on a big belt sander like this. It takes only about 15 minutes, and shouldn't cost more than $50 or so.

handed it over to a worker at the shop. He did the rest, in about 20 minutes time, handing me back a perfectly flat slab, sanded to about 100-grit or so.

one slab, two tables

Learn to sand and finish a big natural slab of wood, and then you'll be able to screw a variety of legs to it. I chose short, round tapered legs—in walnut, just like the slab—to create a great coffee table. For the desk design, I simply chose longer hairpin steel legs. Both leg styles are Mid-Century Modern, which looks good in almost any setting.

Both sets of legs are also available in various sizes. With shorter hairpins and a smaller slab, you can make a coffee table or even a small stool. The same goes for the tapered wood legs: They come in a few different sizes and in a few different woods, to suit almost any slab or top you make.

Speaking of tops, a live-edge slab is not the only way to go with these add-on legs. You could use a butcher-block top—either new or salvaged from an old work-bench or countertop. Or you can use any collection of boards, if you have the skill to join them together.

Let's start with the slab. Once you find one and get it sanded and finished, the rest is easy.

WALNUT IS A GREAT CHOICE. Sometimes called black walnut, this wonderful wood is available in slab form in many parts of the United States and usually has gorgeous grain.

HOW TO HANDLE A BIG SLAB

Here's how to turn any wood slab into a beautiful finished tabletop.

1 CUT OFF THE WASTE. Draw a centerline and then use a big carpenter's framing square to mark where you want to cut off the ends. The square will ensure that the two ends are square to the overall tabletop and parallel with each other. This is also a chance to cut off defects you don't want in the finished top. **2 USE YOUR SAW GUIDE.** The saw guide works with your circular saw to deliver clean, straight cuts so you don't have a ton of sanding and smoothing to do on the ends. **3 A TRICK FOR THICKER SLABS.** If the slab is extra thick, your motor might bottom out on the fence of your saw guide and stop you from setting the blade deep enough. So just use the thin edge of the guide as your straightedge, with the saw riding on the actual wood. Measure the distance from the edge of the base plate to the blade, and then clamp the guide that far away from your line and make the cut with the saw riding against the edge of the guide as shown. **4 FROM ROUGH TO SMOOTH.** A wide-belt sander (see the photo on p. 113) reveals the pretty colors and patterns under the roughsawn surface. A few more passes and this side is done.

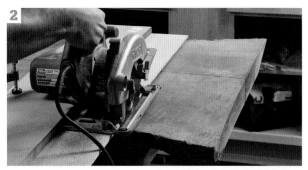

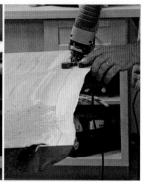

5 BAG THE BARK. You might be tempted to keep the bark on the slab, but it will eventually fall off, leaving the edge unfinished looking. So get rid of it now. Use some kind of scraper to pry it off and then clean up the edge with sandpaper. Notice that we left a few sawmarks on this side when smoothing this slab, because it will be the bottom of the table. That's because I wanted as much thickness as possible.

6 GREAT TRICK FOR RESHAPING AN EDGE. If the edges of your slab are too sharp, like these, or damaged, they are easy to reshape. Just draw a line along one of the grain lines, angle your jigsaw blade to the new angle you want, and cut along the line. **7 NEW NATURAL.** The new edge looks as real as the original one. A bit of sanding will smooth away the sawmarks.

SANDING AND FINISHING THE SLAB

1 SANDING TIPS. On the end grain, you'll need to get rid of the burn marks from the saw by starting with rough sandpaper. Use a block as you work up through the grits to 220-grit. On the curvy edges, back up your sandpaper with a piece of flexible rubber if you have it, working up to 150-grit. Go up to 150-grit on the top too, but use your sanding block or a random-orbit sander. Look how awesome this slab is starting to look!

2 FINAL TOUCHES BEFORE FINISHING. Break all the sharp edges to make them friendly to hands and arms later. Use rough sandpaper at first to make tiny roundovers, and then smooth those edges with finer paper.

3 THICK TABLETOP FINISH. Follow the same steps you used on the plywood coffee table in the last chapter, using three or four coats of oil-based polyurethane and sanding with 220-grit paper between coats. On the ends, sand between coats with 320-grit paper for a buttery feel. Elevate the slab while applying finish so you can reach the edges easily. **4 MAGIC.** The polyurethane reveals the inner beauty of this slab. You never know what you'll find. This beautiful rippled grain was a total bonus, but the rainbow of amazing colors is what I've come to expect from walnut. This is why you are better off buying nice woods than trying to apply wood stain to cheaper ones. You'll never match this natural beauty.

HAIRPIN LEGS ARE DIRT-SIMPLE

These legs come with the screws you need. All you have to do is decide where to place the legs, and then drill some pilot holes. I went for a 4-in. overhang at the ends of the tabletop when placing the legs. That looked about right.

1 MARK A CENTERLINE. Measure to find the center of the underside of the slab, and then use your combo square and long ruler to mark a long centerline down the middle. **2 LOCATE THE LEGS.** Use the square to mark end lines for the leg brackets. Then sit each leg on that line and measure an even distance out from the centerline to the end of the leg bracket and trace the far edge as shown. **3 DRILL AND DRIVE.** Hold the leg brackets on their layout lines and drill pilot holes for each screw. Drive each screw and move on to the next hole. When the legs are all attached, your desk is done!

SUPPLIES

Screw-on hairpin legs
- I-Semble® 3-Rod Hairpin Legs, 4-Pack, Black
- Item No. 54474
- www.rockler.com

WOOD LEGS NEED FINISHING FIRST

These legs and brackets aren't cheap, but they are beautiful and come in four different woods. Pick the bracket size that fits under the slab you have. The brackets and legs are just as easy to attach as the hairpin legs, but they need a few coats of the same finish I used on the tabletop.

1 A FEW COATS OF FINISH. Start with the brackets, elevating them on some boards so you can reach the edges easily. Then brush finish on the legs, screwing them partway into the brackets before touching them up and smoothing any drips. Sand between coats, just as on the slab. **2 INSTALLATION IS EASY.** Mark guidelines near the ends of the slab, as you did for the hairpin legs, and then center the brackets side to side. The screws are "self-tapping," meaning they have a tiny drilling tip, so they don't need pilot holes. Notice how beautifully made these parts are. **3 BRACKETS BARELY SHOW.** The brackets have beveled edges so they look sleek and unobtrusive on the bottom of the table.

SUPPLIES

Tapered wood legs

- McCobb Coffee Table Legs, 16 in., in black walnut, with hanger bolts installed (for a separate charge)

- Item No: LC-MCCB-16-SM

- Angled Cleats and Leg Bolt Installation, 16 in., in black walnut

- Item No: SL-ANGL-16-SM

- Both from www.tablelegs.com

add IKEA legs to anything

Go on www.IKEA.com and you'll find they sell all of their table legs as separate items, and all of them simply screw onto any top you have. There is a wide range of designs to choose from, all much cheaper than the legs I used on the slab. I harvested mine from an old IKEA desk, and added them to a simple plywood top to create a much-needed deck table.

REDUCE, REUSE, RECYCLE. I harvested my legs from an old IKEA desk we were getting rid of.

ANOTHER THICK TOP

I made this top like the one I made for the workstation in Chapter 2, but I used plywood this time, with glue between the layers for extra strength. I started with two 4-ft. by 4-ft. pieces of construction-grade plywood from the home center, to keep the price down, but made sure at least one piece had a good-looking side.

1 HOLES FOR SCREWS. I used screws again to attach the bottom layer to the top one, so I needed another grid of clearance holes and countersinks. I put a layer of the rigid foam underneath to drill into. The pencil line is where I planned to cut off the top, so no screws needed to go there. **2 LAYER OF GLUE.** Unlike the workstation top, this one won't be supported by a cabinet, so I rolled on some wood glue to make sure the top ended up extra-strong. **3 SCREWS AS CLAMPS.** I love this technique. By screwing up from the bottom, you are clamping the two layers together firmly while the glue dries. **4 TRIM AND ROUT.** After a few hours, I trimmed a bit off each edge with the saw guide, just to make them all flat and even. And I trimmed a lot off one side to create the rectangle I wanted. Then I sanded the edges smooth and routed a roundover on the top and bottom, using the same bit from earlier in this book.

5 **THREE COATS OF FINISH.** I used three coats of spar varnish, which will resist sun and rain better than normal polyurethane. I sanded between coats as usual.   **6** **LEGS SCREW ON IN SECONDS.** I spaced them equally from the edges, drilled pilot holes, and drove screws. Couldn't be simpler.   **7** **PERFECT PATIO TABLE FOR $40.** I only had to pay for the plywood, but the four legs would have added less than $20 total if I had to buy them.

8

floating shelves are an engineering marvel

HANGING IN SPACE. The shelves have no visible means of support, yet can hold a surprising amount of weight.

A LOT OF THE fun of building stuff is in the engineering. In fact, every successful project is a feat of problem solving and basic physics.

Consider the projects in this book. The outdoor bench transfers your weight across the seat, down through the uprights, to the earth below, keeping your butt suspended 18 in. off the ground. The bottle opener suspends something in midair too—this time a pile of metal caps, held there with a rare earth magnet, hidden behind the wood.

This chapter's project is another engineering trick, and one that's maybe even more likely to impress your friends. By using the right materials and combining them in a specific way, you can make a stack of shelves that hang on a wall with no visible means of support. If people look very closely, they might figure it out, but most won't—until you explain it to them.

Here's a tip from an experienced bragger: Keep it short! You'll lose your audience if you get long-winded. They are already impressed—don't ruin it!

PLAIN OR PAINTED. The thin plywood edges look fine under an oil finish. Or you can paint them like I did on the previous page.

EVERY MATERIAL HAS ITS STRENGTHS

What I love about this project—aside from the simple physics, and how clean the shelves look on the wall— is how it makes use of the specific properties of solid wood and plywood. Each shelf is a hollow box, made by sandwiching thin plywood or MDF over a few sticks of solid wood. You might be tempted to make the outer skins from solid wood, too, because you can buy thin pieces at your home center. Don't do it.

You'll be attaching a cleat to the wall, which fits into the back of each hollow shelf box, and then a row of screws go down through the top layer into the cleat. If those screws went through a thin piece of solid wood, the wood would split along the grain, sending your collection of My Little Ponies® crashing to the ground. But plywood and MDF are different. They are strong in every direction, which is just what you need for these thin skins.

What's also cool is how a thin-walled box can be so strong. The box will definitely flex if you squeeze it, but try pulling it apart along its length or width. You can't do it. This is the same principle used in

FLOATING SHELVES ARE AN ENGINEERING MARVEL

airplane construction to create thin-skinned, feather-light components that would be easy to dent with a hammer but are impossible to pull apart. That's how the Wright brothers made a wood-and-cloth contraption fly. Today the cloth is high-grade aluminum and the sticks are a honeycomb of even more exotic metals.

We do need some strength at the edges of our shelves to hold those skins together, and small strips of solid wood are just the thing. Together with some yellow glue and firm, even pressure, those strips complete a box that is as strong as an airplane wing. For the geeks out there, it's called a torsion box.

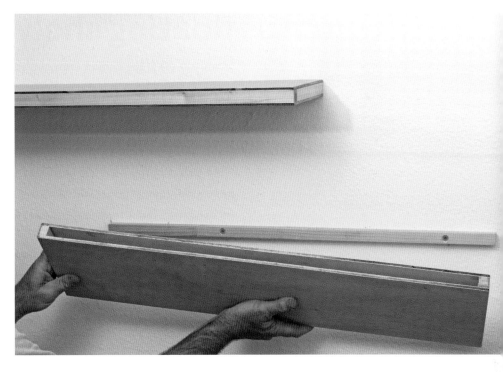

TORSION BOX. The secret is in the hollow box . . . and the solid-wood cleat attached to the wall.

A PRIMAL IMPULSE

Building things is all about mastering the forces of the universe. You can feel them moving through your jigsaw, drill, or handsaw. Learning to harness those forces is learning to cooperate with nature, learning how to align your intent with the world around you.

You aren't the first to feel powerful in this way. Building and creating is an impulse that is as old as our species. When you feed it you touch something deep in your DNA, naturally selected by a million years of evolution and survival. These floating shelves are not so different from the work we once did with bark, logs, skins, and stone. We love solving engineering problems because it's in our primal memory.

If you're not picking up what I'm laying down, that's fine. You can still enjoy these floating shelves. They're cool.

10

floating shelves

As you can see in the photos, these shelves can be made thick or thin, painted or not. At first I thought just oiling them would look bad, because the edges of the plywood would show through. But the thin plywood edges ended up looking like a stripey border along the top and bottom, and not in a bad way. So the woody look was born.

But a stack of these shelves also looks great under a couple of bright coats of some funky color of normal acrylic or milk paint. To make the bigger shelves for my daughter's room, I went with thicker MDF skins for the top and bottom. MDF takes paint beautifully, but wouldn't look so great under the oil finish.

MDF always matches its stated thickness, whereas plywood is a bit thinner than advertised. So 1/4-in. MDF is considerably thicker than "1/4-in." plywood, making the painted shelf thicker and also able to bear more weight.

For the thicker MDF shelves, I also used a wider stick for the wall cleat. This let me place the screws that go down through the back edge farther away from the wall, leaving more MDF there to stop the screws from tearing out under a heavy load.

As for the solid wood strips in the center, you can buy them in all sizes at your local home center. I used both square and rectangular sticks here, making sure they were the same thickness. I went with poplar over pine, because the former is a bit harder and holds screws more firmly.

CHOP UP YOUR MATERIALS

1 PLYWOOD FIRST. Use the saw guide from Chapter 2 to cut the thin plywood (or MDF) to width, resting it on rigid foam insulation to make safe cuts. Then stack the parts and cut them to length on the miter saw. Be sure all the pieces are pushed firmly against the rear fence before cutting.

With thin skins on the top and bottom and solid strips at the edges, you are creating a super-light yet very strong box. The back strip is left out, creating a box that is hollow at the back. When the cleat is screwed into the wall studs, the hollow box is slipped over it, and you drive a few screws down into the cleat, the shelf is surprisingly solid. That's the principle, and the sizes and the thickness of the materials can vary for shelves of all sizes.

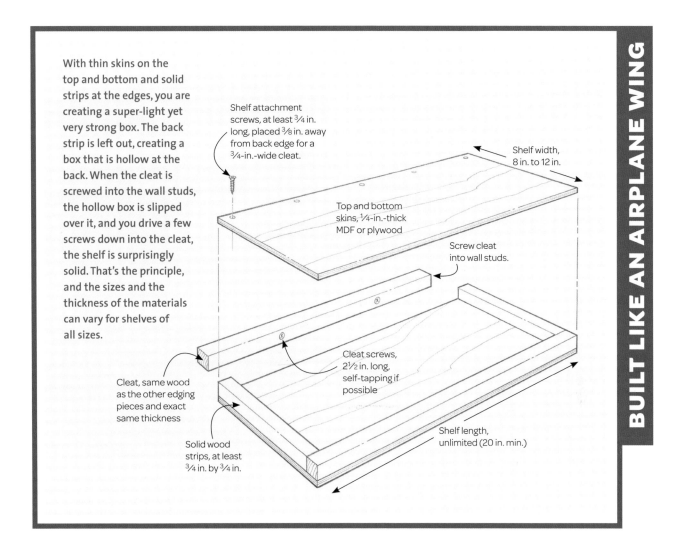

Shelf attachment screws, at least ¾ in. long, placed ⅜ in. away from back edge for a ¾-in.-wide cleat.

Top and bottom skins, ¼-in.-thick MDF or plywood

Screw cleat into wall studs.

Shelf width, 8 in. to 12 in.

Cleat, same wood as the other edging pieces and exact same thickness

Cleat screws, 2½ in. long, self-tapping if possible

Solid wood strips, at least ¾ in. by ¾ in.

Shelf length, unlimited (20 in. min.)

2 CHECK YOUR SOLID WOOD. Lay down all your wood strips to find the sides that are the same thickness (they often vary) and mark those with a check. Then chop them to length on the miter saw.

ASSEMBLE THE FRONT OF THE BOX FIRST

Start by gluing the long front strip between the two layers of plywood. As I mentioned when gluing parts for the outdoor bench, yellow glue needs a few things to do its job well: Use enough of it, spread it evenly, and apply firm, even pressure.

1 THE BRAD TRICK. To keep the wood pieces from sliding around as I clamped them to the plywood, I drove tiny ½-in.-long brads into them, and then clipped off the heads with a wire cutter, which is part of my needlenose pliers. Do the same on the other side of the strips, resting the bottom-side nails on something soft.   **2 LONG STRIP DOWN.** Squirt on plenty of glue, and then spread it along the joint area. Align the long wood strip carefully and push the brads on its underside down into the plywood below.   **3 FINISH THE SANDWICH.** Now spread more glue on top of the strip and add the top piece of plywood, aligning it carefully as you push it down onto the top row of clipped brads.   **4 LOTS OF CLAMPS.** Even with the clamping cauls in place, I used a lot of clamps, trying to leave less than 4 in. or so between them.

CLAMPING CAULS SPREAD PRESSURE

No matter how many clamps you have, whenever you are clamping down a long piece of thin material you need some sort of stiff clamping pad to distribute the pressure and make it even and strong along the whole joint.

A FEW EXTRA STRIPS DO THE TRICK.
I used a couple more of my solid wood strips to spread the clamp pressure.

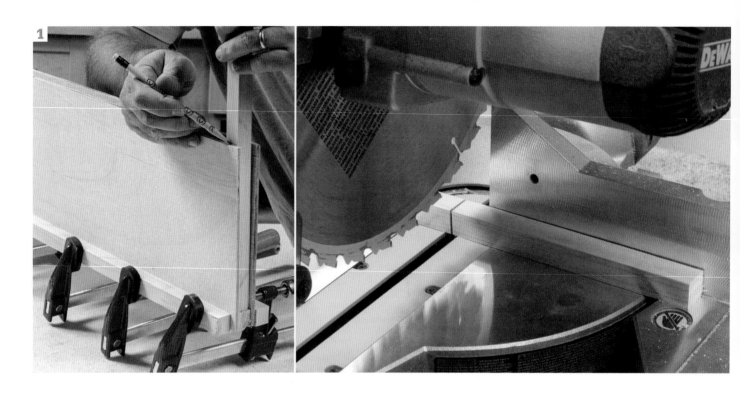

A BETTER GLUE BRUSH

I like to use "flux" brushes to spread glue. I learned from fellow furniture maker Michael Fortune how to make those brushes work better.

HAMMER AND TRIM. Pound on the part that grabs the bristles, and fewer of them will fall out into the glue. Then trim the long bristles to make the brush stiffer and more effective for the job.

1 CUT THE SIDE STRIPS. Mark the length of these by fitting them into their spaces, and then cut them to the mark. **2 EASY TO GLUE IN.** The short side strips won't slide around when clamped so no brads are needed. Just spread on some glue, push the strip down into place, and start clamping from the bottom up. Put the clamps closer together than before and you won't need clamping cauls here. **3 LAST STRIP.** Do the same thing at the other end of the box, adding the last side strip. **4 SIZE THE CLEAT.** Take one more strip and stick it into the hollow at the back of the box to mark its length. A little short is good.

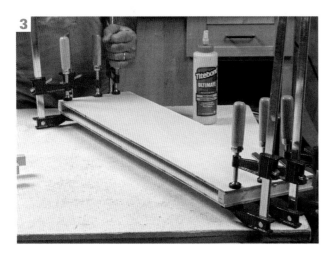

TRIM AND FINISH THE SHELF

1 TRIM THE FRONT EDGE OF THE BOX. At this point you'll likely have some misalignment at the edges, as well as some dried glue that has squeezed out, but it's easy to trim off a hair and clean up all the sides. Use your saw guide to trim the front edge of the box (and the back edges if needed). Notice that I had to put an extra shelf under the back of the saw guide to support it. **2 TRIM THE ENDS, TOO.** You could use the saw guide here also, but it's easier to clean up the ends with a light cut on the miter saw. **3 SAND THEM SMOOTH.** The final prep for finishing or painting is sanding away all the sawmarks on the edges, working from 120-grit up to 220-grit paper and using your sanding block, and then putting a nice, light bevel on the corners with 150-grit paper. **4 CHOOSE YOUR FINISH.** I took a chance on an oil finish here, and even the exposed edges of the plywood came out looking great. But you can also paint these shelves.

FLOATING SHELVES ARE AN ENGINEERING MARVEL

INSTALLATION TIME

The shelves are super-easy to hang on the wall. The keys are to be sure you are screwing into the studs inside the wall, and then leveling the cleats and spacing them evenly to create a nice array.

1 STUD FINDER. Once you know where your shelves are going, you can just knock on the walls and wait for the hollow sound to change to a dull thunk to find studs. But it's easier to use an inexpensive stud finder. Mark the spot and drive in a test screw to be sure. You can always try another spot if they will all be hidden behind the shelf.
2 DRILL CLEARANCE HOLES. Drill holes through the cleat (but not farther) for the big screws to pass through. I used a combo bit that also countersinks. **3 ATTACH THE CLEAT LEVEL.** Drive a 2¹/₂-in.-long screw through one clearance hole at the stud mark on the wall. Then put a level on the cleat and drill the clearance hole and drive a screw at the next stud mark. If the screw doesn't find a stud, you can move it to one side or the other with no problem.

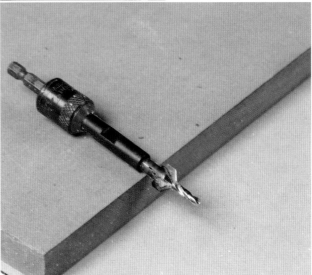

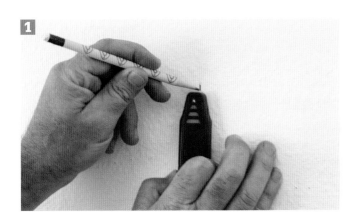

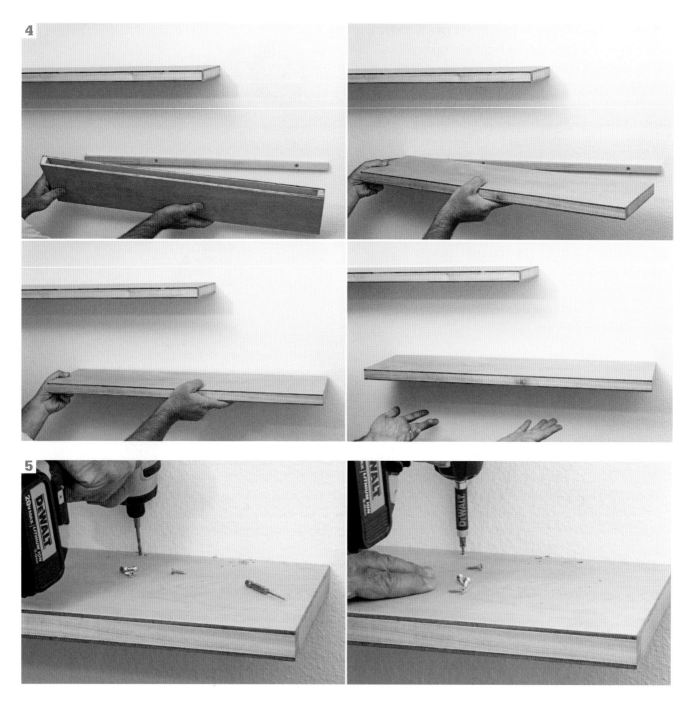

4 **LEVITATION.** The hollow shelf fits tightly over the cleat and hangs in space before you even drive the first screw to attach it. **5** **HIDDEN SCREWS LOCK IT ON THE WALL.** Push the shelf firmly against the wall and drill clearance holes only through the plywood skin but no farther. Then drill smaller pilot holes down into the wood cleat below and drive screws down flush with the surface of the plywood. A casual observer will never see them.

FLOATING SHELVES ARE AN ENGINEERING MARVEL

9 let your light shine

WARM GLOW. The light shines through the thin wood veneer, highlighting the grain and your woodworking skills at the same time. With this notched-frame construction, you can design lamps of all shapes and sizes.

IF YOU NEVER TRY to build a lamp or lighting fixture of some kind, you're missing out on a world of fun. There are whole Web sites devoted to the parts and pieces you'll need: cords, plugs, sockets, LEDs, and so much more. Even your local home center now carries old-timey Edison bulbs with glowing filaments. And you can make the fixtures from all sorts of things, from old bottles to our friend from an earlier chapter, plumbing pipes.

But the subject of this book is wood, so wood it is for the hanging lamp in this chapter. That's no apology. Wood, cut super thin, is an amazing material for lamp shades. We'll use precut strips of thin wood veneer to create the louvered shade on this light, and we'll take advantage of the unique properties of plywood too.

Without plywood, I couldn't have made the internal frame. That's because plywood is made of "plies"—thin layers of wood with grain running in alternating directions. That construction makes plywood strong in every direction.

Solid wood, on the other hand, has grain that travels in one direction, up and down the tree. That's why it is much stronger along its length than across the grain. By the way, this is how those "karate masters" are able to break boards at the county fair. Look closely and you'll see they've cut the boards so the grain is running in the short direction. Any 10-year-old with a temper could break that beefy timber.

If you made this internal frame from solid wood, some of the narrower areas would have the wrong grain orientation and be prone to snapping off. Plywood, on the other hand, turns those corners without breaking stride. By the way, I would avoid MDF for these internal parts. It won't be as strong as plywood in the narrow areas. Plus it's a bit heavier.

A NEW MATERIAL TO TRY OUT

The other material that makes this lamp possible is wood veneer, in this case cherry. You could use any hardwood veneer (softwoods like pine might be too fragile), but cherry is perfect. It's beautiful on its own and gives off an awesome glow when light passes through it.

A lot of people think cherry is a dark reddish color, but that's because factory furniture manufacturers create a fake "cherry" look by staining cheaper woods. This veneer is the real thing, a light, creamy brown with a hint of red. One coat of oil finish brings it to life.

By buying a roll of precut 2-in.-wide strips (called edge-banding because it's normally used to hide the edges of plywood), I was able to avoid cutting long,

PRECUT VENEER. Thin 2-in.-wide strips of veneer are the perfect material for the louvered rings of the lamp.

perfect strips of veneer from a big sheet. But you can cut your own strips if you can't find the precut stuff, using a straightedge and a sharp utility knife. If you do, glue sandpaper to the underside of your straightedge so it doesn't slip as you make multiple light passes with the knife.

A lot of the edge-banding you'll find online comes preglued, with an iron-on adhesive. I would avoid that for this project. It will probably make the thin veneer less translucent, and it might get melty if the lightbulb gets hot.

ALL CREDIT TO CHRIS BECKSVOORT AND *FINE WOODWORKING*

The genesis of this design lies in the fertile brain of a legendary craftsman in rural Maine. Christian H. Becksvoort is not only the leading custom maker of authentic Shaker furniture; he also designs modern pieces similar to this one. In a past life, as editor of *Fine Woodworking* magazine, I published Becksvoort's version of a pendant lamp, and tucked it away in my mind palace as a project for later.

When I started picking projects for this book, Chris's lamp came to mind, but I wasn't about to just copy it. For one thing, he used a bandsaw and a lathe to make his, two woodworking machines that don't fit the scope of this book. But a straight copy would be lame anyway. So I redesigned his creation, simplifying the construction and turning his elegant onion shape into a wide V.

Then I placed a call from coast to coast to make sure my old friend would be OK with me borrowing some of his hard-won inspiration. He liked the book's

mission and gave a quick yes. He's a prince of a guy, like most woodworkers.

By the way, you can see both of us briefly in an episode of the NBC comedy *Parks and Recreation,* titled "Ron and Diane," courtesy of our mutual friend Nick Offerman, who got us written into the show for a few moments way back when. Talk about 15 minutes of fame—it was more like 5 seconds. Strangely, Hollywood never came calling for me and Chris again, whereas Nick works constantly.

I have to give a shout-out to *Fine Woodworking,* too, which has been documenting the work of brilliant makers like Chris Becksvoort for 40 years and counting.

the power of the subconscious mind

Back to my mind palace. When I was simplifying Becksvoort's design so it could be built using only the basic tools covered in this book, I started with a sketch, thinking through each of the steps, sleeping on some of the problems—and waking up with solutions in the morning, or two days later.

It's amazing how your subconscious mind continues to solve problems while your conscious brain is occupied with other things. Recent brain studies prove that this is true. In fact, taking a break from a problem is often the key to solving it. Forget about the problem, put down your smartphone, go on a long walk or bike ride, get some sleep, and let your subconscious take over. There are deep regions of your brain that will easily outmaneuver your frontal lobe.

When Elias Howe was struggling to perfect the mechanical sewing machine in the 1840s, he slept on the problem and had a strange dream. In it, cannibals were threatening him with long spears, each one with a hole at the tip. Howe had found the needle he needed.

Of course, Howe had to try out his weird idea to be sure it actually worked, and I had to do that too with my lamp design. When I started cutting

UNDERRATED PLAYER. Equipped with upgraded blades for extra-clean cuts in wood, the affordable jigsaw will make amazingly smooth straight and curved cuts, rivaling those made on a big, expensive bandsaw. Just avoid sideways pressure on the blade, which will make it flex and cut on an angle.

out the plywood shapes, notching the toy wheels, and screwing the pieces together, I had more troubleshooting to do, but soon I had a working prototype, made with the same basic tool kit we've been using all along.

One thing I hope you get from this book is that it's not always about the tools you own. Success, and fun, is more about being creative with what you have.

THE POWER OF THE JIGSAW

The jigsaw is overlooked by a lot of woodworkers, who jump right to a bandsaw that costs $500 or more. But the humble jigsaw can do amazing things. Armed with a long, smooth-cutting blade designed for hardwoods, it made beautifully straight cuts in the 1/2-in.-thick plywood, so the veneer rings had flat landing spots. It

also made perfect little cuts in the wood wheels, for the sides of the notches. But then I ran into a problem: How do I chop out the waste in the middle of each notch?

The furniture maker in me knew that I could finish off the notches with some deft chisel work, but I'm saving handplanes, chisels, and the careful sharpening they require for a future stage of your journey. After some head-scratching, I had an "oh, duh" moment, realizing I could just load one of the narrowest blades in the jigsaw and make tiny curved cuts in each notch that would chop out the waste and leave a flat bottom.

My backup plan would have been to introduce a new hand tool, the inexpensive but handy coping saw, but I'll save that one for later too. There's more than one way to skin a lamp. Speaking of that, if you do happen to own a bandsaw, that machine will make it even easier to cut out the frame pieces and notch the wooden wheels.

hanging lamp with a veneer shade

Armed with the approach shown here, you can design lamps of all shapes and sizes. And with all the lamp supplies available online, you could turn any of those hanging designs into a table lamp too. The core of the construction is a pair of wood wheels, sold for toy building. Those get small notches, which anchor four identical plywood frames. These in turn support a series of veneer rings that wrap around the outside. Every house needs a foundation, and the wheels were the key. They even come with predrilled axle holes, perfect for the lamp cord to pass through.

MATERIALS & SUPPLIES

- ½-in. plywood, 2 ft. by 4 ft. panel
- Wood veneer edge-banding, 2 in. wide, non-glued, at least 30 ft. long (I got mine on eBay®)
- Wooden toy wheels, flat, ³⁄₄ in. thick by 2³⁄₈ in. dia., from www.leevalley.com (Item 41K01.17)
- Drywall screws, 1¼ in. long
- 12 ft. of rayon-covered lamp cord, with toggle switch, from www.1000bulbs.com
- Short keyless socket, 3-piece, from www.1000bulbs.com
- LED bulb, 60-watt equivalent, omnidirectional (LED bulbs run cooler, which is better inside this wood frame)

The frame is made of four identical pieces, notched into wood wheels at the top and bottom. Those are identical too. Then you make big rings from strips of veneer, and simply glue them onto the frame. The lamp cord goes through a hole in the top wheel and the bulb just hangs in the middle of the frame.

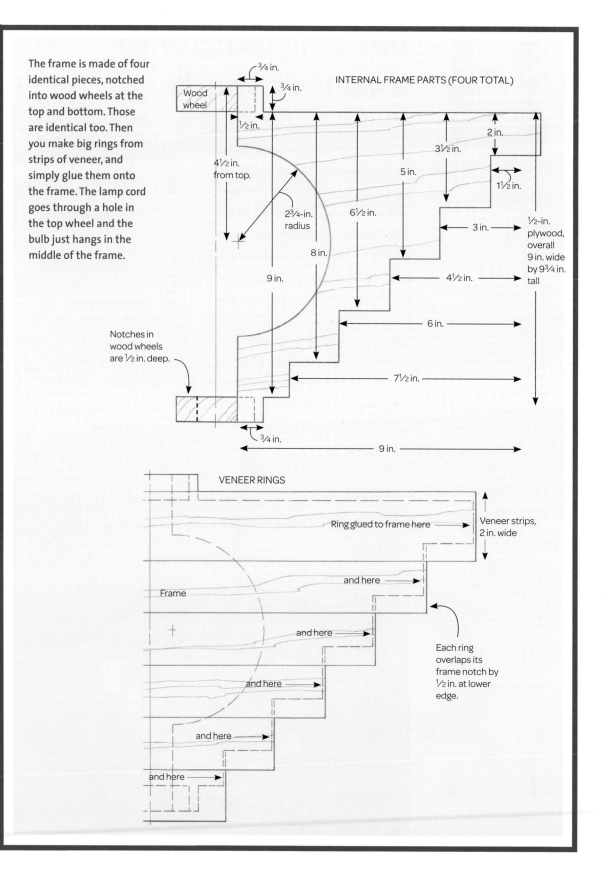

INTERNAL FRAME PARTS (FOUR TOTAL)

¾ in.

¾ in.

Wood wheel

½ in.

4½ in. from top.

2¾-in. radius

2 in.

3½ in.

5 in.

1½ in.

½-in. plywood, overall 9 in. wide by 9¾ in. tall

6½ in.

3 in.

8 in.

9 in.

4½ in.

6 in.

Notches in wood wheels are ½ in. deep.

7½ in.

¾ in.

9 in.

VENEER RINGS

Ring glued to frame here

Veneer strips, 2 in. wide

Frame

and here

and here

Each ring overlaps its frame notch by ½ in. at lower edge.

and here

and here

and here

CUT AND LAY OUT THE FRAME PARTS

After cutting plywood squares for the four frame parts, you need to lay out their notches as precisely as possible, so put on some tunes, sharpen your pencil, and let it flow.

1 CHOP UP YOUR PLYWOOD. Each of the four identical plywood frame parts starts as a rectangle. Use the saw guide from earlier in the book to cut your big plywood panel into the pieces you need. **2 LAY OUT THE NOTCHES.** Your combo square is the perfect tool here. To make a line parallel to an edge, just slide the square and pencil at the same time. To mark two sides of a notch at once, use both the end and the edge of the ruler. **3 LAY OUT THE ARCS.** These lighten the frames and make room for the bulb. Mark the center point as close to the edge as possible, and then trace the arc with a compass of some kind.

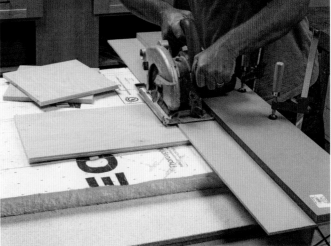

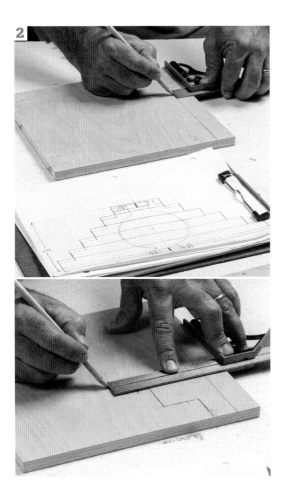

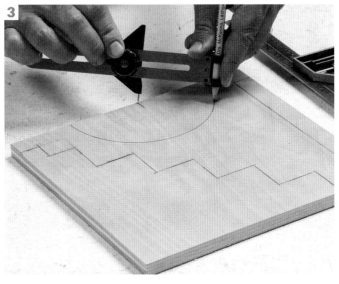

SMOOTH JIGSAWING

Use that smooth-cutting blade for the jigsaw from the bottle-opener project, and stay on the right side of the line!

1 SAW THE NOTCHES. Do all the cuts in one direction before changing your angle and finishing each cutout. **2 NOW THE CIRCLES.** Cut out the semicircles. These don't have to be perfect, but it's fun to try anyway. **3 FLAT AND LEVEL.** Feel free to smooth all of the surfaces, but the most important ones are the small flats where the veneer rings will be glued on. To get all the way into the corner of the notch, move the sandpaper right up to the edge of the block. Then rock the block to make sure it is flat on the surface before starting to sand. Don't go for perfection; just flatten it a bit.

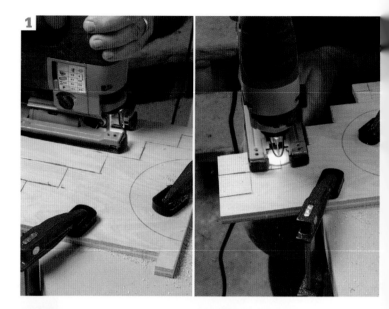

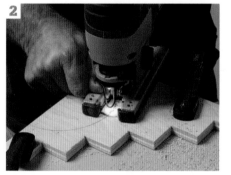

USE A HAND SCREW TO MAKE A VISE

Buy a couple of these old carpenter's clamps and you won't be sorry. Here's just one way they solve problems.

CLAMP THE CLAMP. Use one of your bar clamps to clamp a hand screw to any work surface.

INSTANT VISE. The hand screw will now lock a board in the vertical position for careful handwork.

WOOD WHEELS ARE THE FOUNDATION ━━━━━━

SHARPEN YOUR PENCIL ON SANDPAPER

When your layout has to be super-accurate, you need to keep your pencil very sharp. Rather than reaching for the pencil sharpener again and again, do what old draftsmen did and sharpen the tip with a few quick swipes on a sanding block.

TRY A CHISEL POINT. Use your sanding block and fine sandpaper to form a super-sharp wedge at the tip. It's fast and foolproof.

Toy wooden wheels make the perfect anchors for the tops and bottoms of the four frames, but only if you notch them carefully.

1 DRAW CENTERLINES. Working by eye, divide each wheel down the middle, using the center hole as your guide, and draw another centerline at a right angle to the first. If the crisscrossing lines look square and centered, they are. If not, make an adjustment.

2 NOW THE BOTTOMS OF THE NOTCHES. Set your square for $1/2$ in. and use the end of the ruler to draw a line at the bottom of each notch.

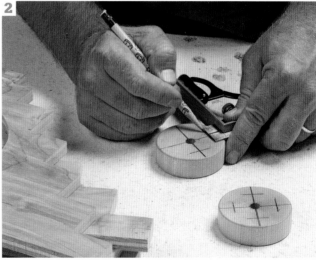

3 USE THE PLYWOOD TO LAY OUT THE NOTCHES. This is easier and more accurate then measuring. Mark a centerline on a small piece of the frame plywood, and use that line to center the plywood on the wheels as you mark both sides of the notches. **4 SAW THE SIDES.** Use your smooth-cutting blade to saw carefully along the inside of the lines, stopping at the bottom of the notch. **5 SWITCH BLADES.** To remove all the waste, switch to a narrow blade that can turn tight corners. **6 TIGHT TURN.** Start in the sawcut that's already there and then turn the corner when you get near the bottom, going straight along the line into the opposite corner.

7 FINISH THE FLAT. Turn the jigsaw around and start with the blade in the flat corner you made. Cut toward the opposite corner to finish the bottom of the notch.

HOLD ROUND OBJECTS WITH A HAND SCREW

To make the curving cuts in the little notches (step 6), you can't have any clamps in the way. To grab the sides of the wood wheels, I notched one of my hand screws as shown. It will still work for other jobs though.

DEEP NOTCHES. Lay these out in pencil and then cut them. Try to leave at least 3/4 in. of wood in the thinnest areas so the tip of the jaws won't snap off.

GREAT GRAB. This is a lesson in using what you have to get the job done.

SCREW AND GLUE THE FRAME PARTS

With the notches done, you can glue the frame parts to the wood wheels, completing the lamp frame. Screws hold the parts in place while the glue dries and add some additional strength.

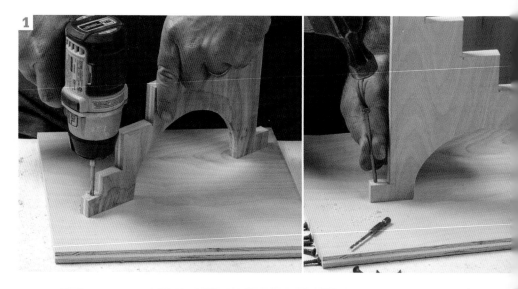

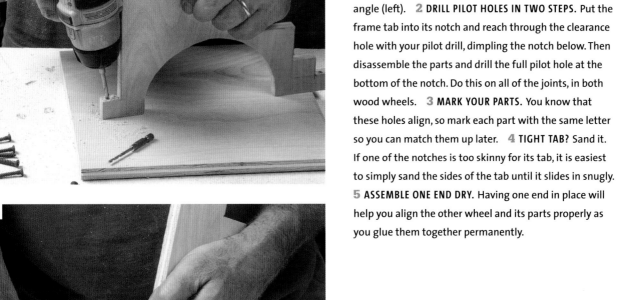

1 DRILL CLEARANCE HOLES. At the stepped end of the frame it is easy to drill (far left). But there isn't much room at the fat end. So you might have to create a center dimple with a nail first (center) so you can drill on a slight angle (left). **2 DRILL PILOT HOLES IN TWO STEPS.** Put the frame tab into its notch and reach through the clearance hole with your pilot drill, dimpling the notch below. Then disassemble the parts and drill the full pilot hole at the bottom of the notch. Do this on all of the joints, in both wood wheels. **3 MARK YOUR PARTS.** You know that these holes align, so mark each part with the same letter so you can match them up later. **4 TIGHT TAB?** Sand it. If one of the notches is too skinny for its tab, it is easiest to simply sand the sides of the tab until it slides in snugly. **5 ASSEMBLE ONE END DRY.** Having one end in place will help you align the other wheel and its parts properly as you glue them together permanently.

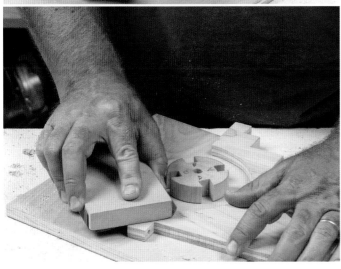

6

PUT YOUR GLUE IN A DISH

Rather than squirting glue straight out of the bottle onto your workpieces where it can drip, it's often easier to squirt some into a lid or other throwaway item and dip your glue brush into that.

THE DISH TRICK. Use a jar lid as a glue reservoir. Then you can dip in your brush, pick up a small amount, and dab that on with great control.

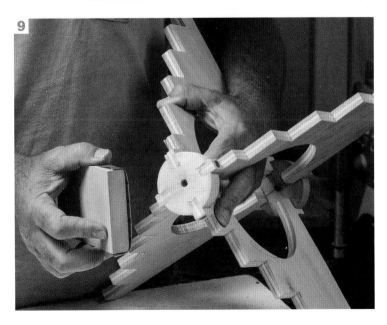

6 APPLY GLUE FOR REAL. With the one end assembled temporarily, you can start applying glue to the other end, first to the sides of the tabs and then to the inside of the notch. **7 PULL IT TIGHT AND DRIVE SCREWS.** Use a clamp to pull all of the joints fully closed, making sure the tabs line up with the top of the wheels. Then drive in 1¼-in.-long screws to lock everything in place. **8 LAST SIDE.** Now unscrew the other end, remove the wood wheel, apply glue to the joints, and drive screws to finish off the lamp frame. **9 A LITTLE MORE SANDING.** People will see the bottom end of the lamp, so sand off the pencil marks and dried glue.

2 CLAMP CAREFULLY. Now bring in the clamp, with the block taped to its far end, and clamp the joint together. Check the pencil line to make sure the joint hasn't moved and adjust the overlap if it has.   **3 LAST LOOP.** Do the same thing to the other strips, down to the smallest one. Let them dry for an hour each and then test-fit them on the frame to see how they all look together. If a ring turns out wrong, just cut a new strip and start again.   **4 LIGHT CLEANUP.** To clean up a small amount of misalignment, sand the edges. Sand the tiny overlap to remove any excess glue and rough edges.

5 SMOOTH FINISH. One coat of oil finish will darken the rings and bring out the beauty of the wood. I used tung oil finish. Wipe on plenty and then wipe off the excess.

WIRING TIME

It's easier to do the wiring now, before attaching all the rings. Start by disassembling the three-part socket. It comes apart easily. (And, of course, make sure that everything's unplugged until the job is completely done.)

1 THREAD THE CORD FIRST. Be sure to run the cord through the upper wheel, and then through the bottom of the socket, before attaching the wires. **2 NOW ASSEMBLE THE SOCKET.** The wires screw onto posts on either side of the inner core. Then the parts slip into each other. Finish by firmly pushing the socket base onto its body.

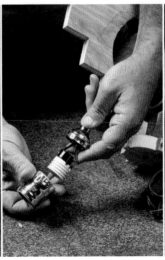

HANGING LAMP WITH A VENEER SHADE

3 A KNOT HANDLES THE PRESSURE. Pull
the socket to free up enough cord to tie a
knot. The knot goes as close to the socket
as possible. When you hang the lamp, the
knot moves up against the upper wheel and
takes all the weight.

GLUE ON THE RINGS ONE BY ONE

Tape on glue blocks when you can, and arrange the clamps any which way to get pressure where you need it. Take a close look at the rings as you attach them, making sure they aren't twisted or bowed out of whack. And be sure to use Titebond III, which will give you more working time before it gets too sticky.

1 APPLY GLUE. Brush a generous amount onto each end of the frame, but only for the ring you are working on. Glue the other notches as you attach their rings. **2 THE FIRST ONE IS TRICKY.** The largest ring just sits on the outer part of the frame, with no notch to guide it. So take it slow and measure to be sure the ring is sticking up from the frame 1/2 in. on all sides (the frame is upside down, so ultimately this will be the bottom edge of the ring). **3 CLAMP ALL FOUR POINTS.** You should be able to thread a second bar clamp under the first, but you might not be able to use blocks this time. That's OK. There won't be that much pressure on these rings, and the joints will be strong enough.

4 ANY MEANS NECESSARY. The ring was slipping a bit, but some tape on the inside corners, where the ring meets the frame, kept things in place while I tightened the clamps. It doesn't take a ton of pressure here, and too much can flex the frame anyway, making the clamps and ring slip sideways. **5 THE REST ARE EASIER.** They drop down onto their notches, which keep them level as you clamp. **6 A FEW TRICKS.** To keep the bars from tilting over and pressing on the thin edges of the rings, stack something inside to support them. When you reach the middle rings, you can use short clamps to grab the inside of the frame, rather than long ones to reach all the way across. **7 TOUCHDOWN.** The last ring slides on. A bit of glue, a couple more clamps, and you are ready for the lighting ceremony. **8 COOL BULB.** Use an omnidirectional LED bulb in this lamp. Omnidirectional means it will shine in every direction, and LED is much cooler than incandescent (even cooler than CFL). I went with an 11-watt LED, which shines like a 60-watt incandescent, making this an accent light, but you could go with a brighter bulb over a table.

9 HANG IT UP. Put one hook in the ceiling where the light will go, and knot the cord around it. Put another ceiling hook near the wall to manage the cord and send it down to the outlet. I used a cord with a toggle switch in it, but an unswitched cord could plug into a switched outlet, or you could even hard wire the lamp into the ceiling so no cord hangs down at all. (If you aren't comfortable doing house wiring, hire an electrician for this last approach.)

10 transforming table will transform your skills

IT'S A LOW TABLE OR A TALL STOOL. This one is table height at 22 in. Make it a bit shorter, say 18 in., for an even comfier stool.

AS I MENTIONED in an earlier chapter, if you want to build things, it's inspiring and useful to delve into design history. You don't have to be an art snob to find amazing ideas that will hit you like a 2×4. That's what happened to me when I encountered the Bauhaus movement.

The Bauhaus was an actual school, not just a school of thought, founded in Germany in 1919 by architect Walter Gropius, who wanted to reconnect fine art with craftsmanship and put soul and beauty back into furniture and architecture. The Bauhaus ideas were revolutionary at the time. Traditionalists did not want to see fine art made functional. They saw it as dumbing down, but Bauhaus saw it as bringing art into real life.

What I love about the movement are the clean lines, the free experimentation with materials and ideas, and the fact that form always follows function. For Bauhaus designers, a functional item is beautiful in itself. The American Shakers felt the same way. Check out Shaker furniture for a homegrown version of elegant simplicity.

TRANSFORM IT. Flip
the table on its side
and use it for storage.
Stack as many as you
like. Build your world.

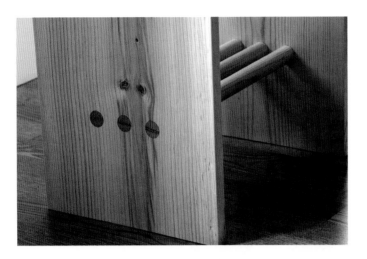

WEDGED TENONS. You can do it. It's old-world joinery: simple and effective.

locking it in place forever. This also means your tenon doesn't have to fit its hole perfectly. The wedging action will spread the tip and fill any gaps.

Plus, once you saw off the excess tenon and the protruding wedge and sand both flush, it looks like you really know what you are doing. Cuz you do. Feel proud.

The thing about the old-time woodworkers was that they needed to move quickly, with rudimentary tools, and wedges were the perfect technology for closing that margin of error. Like I said earlier, woodworkers have been solving the same problems for centuries. What I didn't mention is that it feels awesome to walk in their footprints.

EMBRACE YOUR MISTAKES

One thing that makers always make is mistakes. So when my ⅜-in. drill bit tore the surrounding wood or blew out the nearby end of the board, I took a breath and found an easy way to fix them, with glue and sawdust.

By the way, pine is soft and a bit fragile, hence the drilling problem; I realized that I should have changed out the standard twist drill bit included with the dowel jig and replaced it with a brad-point bit of the same size. Next time.

The big lesson here is to go easy on yourself, let mistakes happen, and realize that each one contains a valuable lesson you won't soon forget.

When I first went to work at *Fine Woodworking* magazine I was pretty freaked out at the prospect of woodworking in front of the more seasoned editors, but the magazine's sage art director, Mike Pekovich, offered some philosophy that I have leaned on ever since. He recommended that I embrace my mistakes, looking at each new project as a record of where I was in my journey at that moment, a sort of personal history.

Turns out that every maker starts at zero, goofing up left and right. Making mistakes means you are trying new things—and learning. Anyway, get used to it. To err is human, someone once said.

PROJECT Nº.

12

transforming table

This table/stool/bookcase is simple and spare, made from a single wide pine board, a row of ⅜-in. dowels at each corner, and a few spindles through the middle. All of the joinery is exposed, putting your crafts-manship on display and add-ing a decorative touch.

MATERIALS

FOR ONE TABLE:

- Pine board, ¾ in. thick by 11¼ in. wide (sold as 1×12) by 6 ft. long.
- Pine dowel, 1 in. dia., 4 ft. long.
- Spiral dowel pins, ⅜ in. dia., from www.rockler.com, $3.50 for a bag of 50

BASIC ANATOMY

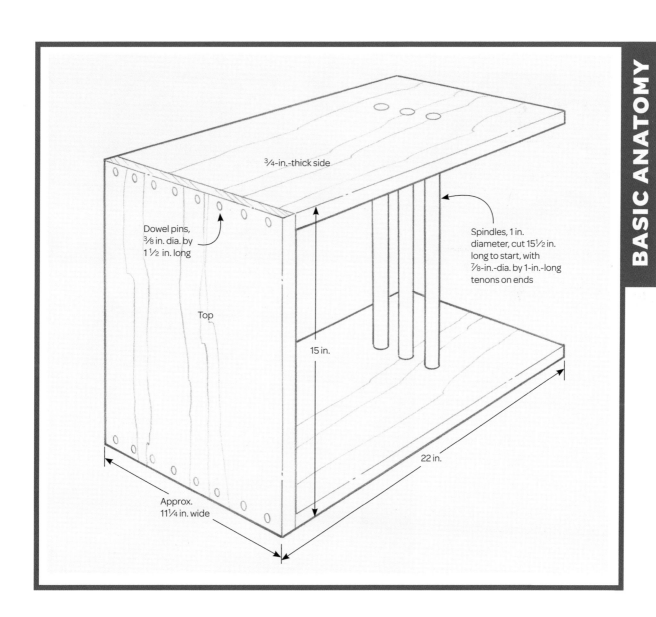

¾-in.-thick side

Dowel pins, ⅜ in. dia. by 1½ in. long

Top

Spindles, 1 in. diameter, cut 15½ in. long to start, with ⅞-in.-dia. by 1-in.-long tenons on ends

15 in.

22 in.

Approx. 11¼ in. wide

CHOP UP A BIG PINE BOARD

You can get both sides and the top from one long, wide, presurfaced pine board, available at lumberyards, home centers, and hardware stores.

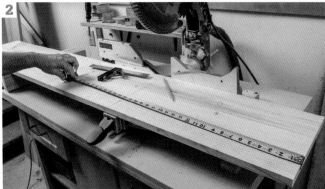

1 LAY OUT PARTS IN SEQUENCE. For a better grain match at the corners, mark out one side, then the top, and then the second side as shown, making marks on the edges to remind you which way they go back together later. **2 CUT THE FIRST PIECE.** Make sure your layout mark is still accurate, and then use the flip trick (see the facing page) to cut the first side of the table. Note that the blade should be on the left side of the line this time! **3 CUT THE REST OF THE PIECES.** Your original layout marks will work for the first piece, but because of the material removed by the blade, your next few layout marks won't be accurate. Measure again and make new marks for the last two parts as you go.

THE FLIP TRICK FOR WIDE BOARDS

There will be boards that are too big for your miter saw to crosscut in one shot, but this trick will let you make a complete crosscut on pieces that are a couple inches too wide.

1 CUT AS FAR AS YOU CAN. Here I am cutting off the rough end of the board, to get a clean, square end to start with. Plunge the saw steadily and let it spin to a stop before lifting it. **2 FLIP AND FIND THE SLOT.** Flip the board over, and drop one tooth of the blade into the end of the slot you just cut. Pay extra attention to the side you are keeping, not the waste side of the slot. **3 ONE MORE CUT.** Now make the rest of the cut. Again, let the blade spin to a stop before lifting it. **4 THE FEEL TEST.** There might be a tiny step between the two cuts. Feel for it with your fingers. If it is too big, you can make a super light cut on the end of the board to remove it, flipping the board whichever way you need to.

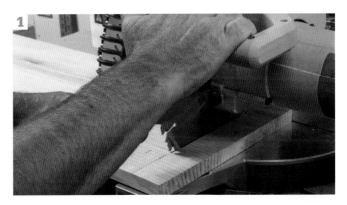

LAY OUT THE DOWEL JOINTS

All you need to make the dowel jig work is small pencil marks. Lay out the dowel spacing on the top of the table, and then just transfer those marks to the two sides.

1 SPACING TRICK. When the width of a piece is an in-between dimension, you can just angle the ruler to make it work. Here the board is 11¼ in. wide, but the angle lets me use the full 12-in. ruler so I can divide the dimensions easily. Now just use a square to carry the marks to the edges where you need them. **2 TRANSFER THE MARKS TO THE OTHER PIECES.** With the top laid out, you can line up the sides as they'll go in the finished piece and transfer the pencil marks over, so you can drill matching holes in mating parts.

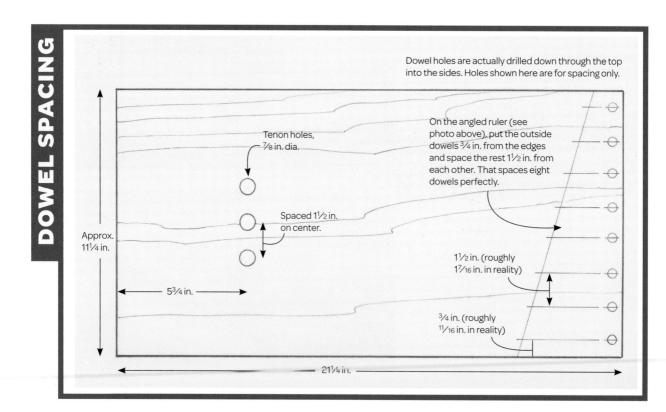

DOWEL SPACING

Dowel holes are actually drilled down through the top into the sides. Holes shown here are for spacing only.

Tenon holes, ⅞ in. dia.

On the angled ruler (see photo above), put the outside dowels ¾ in. from the edges and space the rest 1½ in. from each other. That spaces eight dowels perfectly.

Spaced 1½ in. on center.

Approx. 11¼ in.

5¾ in.

1½ in. (roughly 1⁷⁄₁₆ in. in reality)

¾ in. (roughly 1¹⁄₁₆ in. in reality)

21¼ in.

SET UP FOR SUCCESS

There are just a few things you need to do before you start drilling.

1 SET UP THE STOP COLLAR. We'll drill dowel holes in the sides first, and those can't be too deep or the 1½-in.-long dowels won't pop out the top of the table. So put the stop collar on the drill, insert the drill in the jig, and set the collar so the full diameter of the bit (not the very tip) sticks out only ½ in. **2 BIT GOES IN THE CHUCK.** My drill only accepts hex-shanked bits, so I need an auxiliary chuck to hold round drill bits like this one. **3 CLAMP DOWN THE WORKPIECE.** Clamp one of the sides to your workstation. (You don't need the extra board below it. I was a bit confused here.)

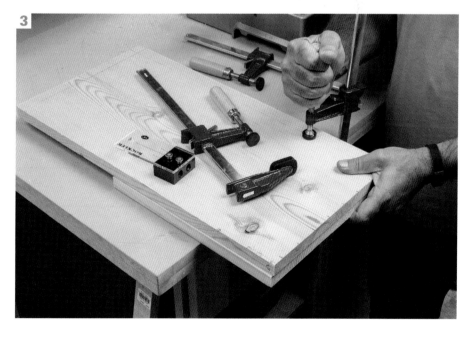

DRILL THE SIDES FIRST

The sides get holes drilled into their ends. The key here is to drill to the right depth, so the right amount of dowel is sticking out.

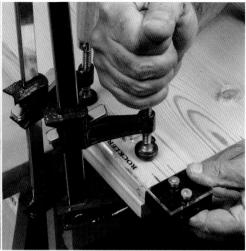

1 EASY ALIGNMENT. There are three alignment marks on the dowel jig: one in the center (which you can ignore) and one on each side, lined up with one of the holes. To line up the jig, just pick one of the outside lines, line it up with a pencil mark on the workpiece, clamp the jig in place while pressing it tightly against the end of the board, and be sure to use that same hole when drilling. **2 SLOW AND STEADY.** The drill might want to grab, so hold it firmly and drill steadily for a clean hole. **3 CHECK THE DEPTH.** Insert a dowel and make sure enough is protruding to get through the top of the table with at least ⅛ in. sticking out. If the depth is wrong, reset the stop collar on the drill bit. **4 DRILL AWAY.** With everything set, you can drill a row of perfect holes in minutes. Find the next layout mark, reposition the jig, drill, repeat.

TRANSFORMING TABLE WILL TRANSFORM YOUR SKILLS

NOW DRILL THE TOP

The holes go down through the edges of the top and out the bottom side, so you don't need the stop collar on the drill bit, but you do need the scrap board underneath, which will stop the underside of the dowel holes from splintering.

1 GET READY. Place the scrap board below the real workpiece. Note that I've wrapped the layout marks around onto the end grain, where I'll be able to see them when the jig is in place. When clamping down the boards, make sure the workpiece sticks out a bit farther than the scrap below it, so the jig can align correctly. **2 GO VERTICAL.** The jig goes upright to drill these holes. You can see why I had to wrap the layout marks onto the end grain. **3 GRAB A LONG CLAMP.** A longer clamp will reach to the far end of the top to clamp the dowel jig in place. **4 SAME AS BEFORE.** Move the jig along as before, realigning and reclamping as you go, to drill another perfect row of holes. If you are getting a lot of blowout around the holes, try switching to a brad-point-type bit of the same size. Brad-point bits are available online.

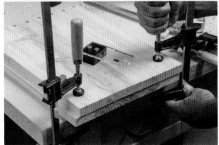

DRILL THE SIDES FOR THE SPINDLES

The 1-in. spindles will have $7/8$-in.-dia. tenons on their ends. Drill holes for those tenons now.

1 LAYOUT IS SIMPLE. Using the drawing on p. 166, mark the location of the holes measuring from the bottom edge of the sides, and square a line across. Then mark the spacing of the holes along that line, starting by finding the center and then spacing the outside holes away from that mark. **2 THE NAIL TRICK.** To make a shallow dent at the center of each hole for accurate drilling, just use a big nail. **3 THE MIGHTY FORSTNER BIT.** No bit drills big holes cleaner than a Forstner bit. Invest in a set if you can. Again, I'm using an auxiliary drill chuck to hold this round-shanked bit. **4 SMOOTH DRILLING.** The Forstner bit will follow the dent you made with the nail, but be sure to keep the bit vertical and square to the workpiece for an accurate hole. Also, you need another scrap board clamped underneath to prevent splintering on the bottom side. **5 CLEAN RESULTS.** Some say you can only use a Forstner bit in a drill press. Don't believe those people. These bits work fine in a handheld drill.

WEDGES ON THE MITER SAW

The miter saw makes short work of these little wedges. They are ⅞ in. wide, like the tenons, so your ¾-in. scraps from the table won't work.

1 USE A 2×4 OR 2×6. With the blade set at 90 degrees, cut a chunk off the end of construction lumber like this 2×6. **2 ANGLE THE BLADE.** Five degrees makes perfect wedges. **3 TURN THE BLOCK AND CUT WEDGES.** Turn the workpiece so the end grain is against the fence and cut a small slice off one corner. Then flip the block and do the same thing at the other three corners.

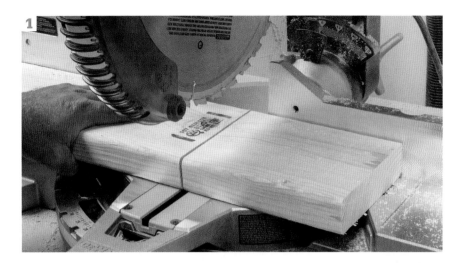

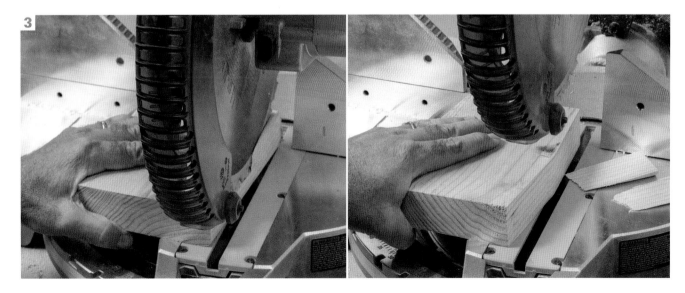

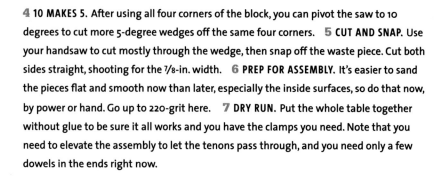

4 10 MAKES 5. After using all four corners of the block, you can pivot the saw to 10 degrees to cut more 5-degree wedges off the same four corners. **5 CUT AND SNAP.** Use your handsaw to cut mostly through the wedge, then snap off the waste piece. Cut both sides straight, shooting for the 7/8-in. width. **6 PREP FOR ASSEMBLY.** It's easier to sand the pieces flat and smooth now than later, especially the inside surfaces, so do that now, by power or hand. Go up to 220-grit here. **7 DRY RUN.** Put the whole table together without glue to be sure it all works and you have the clamps you need. Note that you need to elevate the assembly to let the tenons pass through, and you need only a few dowels in the ends right now.

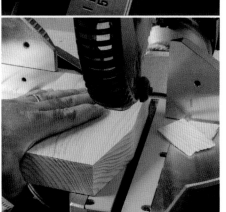

TRANSFORMING TABLE WILL TRANSFORM YOUR SKILLS

SPINDLES GO IN FIRST

The keys to success with this glue-up are using Titebond III, which gives you more working time before it starts drying, and doing the assembly in the right order. Stage one is inserting the spindles and wedging them in place.

1 SPINDLES FIRST. Put the glue in a dish of some kind and brush a liberal coat onto the insides of the holes. Then insert one end of each spindle. **2 NOW THE OTHER SIDE.** Put glue in the other holes and then wiggle the spindles around to get the opposite side of the table to drop onto the tenons. **3 CLAMP CAREFULLY.** Use clamps to make sure the tenons are fully seated, with no gaps at the inside shoulders. Then use a couple of dowels to put the tabletop in place temporarily. If the sides seem misaligned at all, twist them by hand to straighten them out. **4 ALIGN THE SLOTS AND GLUE THE WEDGES.** Note that the slots are all horizontal. That is important. If they went the other way, in line with the grain in the sides, the wedging action could split those boards! Brush some glue onto the sides of the wedges.
5 BANG 'EM IN AND LISTEN. Just like your crafty ancestors did, use a hammer to tap in the wedges until the banging sound becomes a dull thud. Then you know the wedges are solid. Now wedge the tenons on the other side, switching the clamps around if you need to. You'll cut off the excess wedge later (see p. 183).

NOW ADD THE TOP

There are stages
to this process too,
which make every-
thing easier.

TRANSFORMING TABLE WILL TRANSFORM YOUR SKILLS

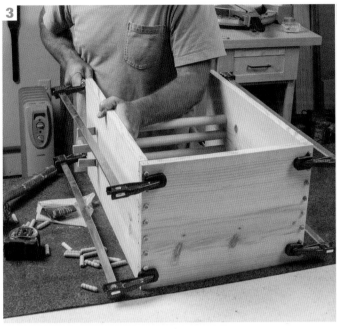

1 DOWELS IN FIRST. Flip the table right side up, and pour some glue in each of the dowel holes. Use a little stick to spread it around inside the holes, and then put in the dowels, giving each one a twist to spread the glue even more.

2 NOW THE TOP. Brush glue onto each of the dowels that are sticking up from the sides, moving as quickly as you can. Then fit the top onto the dowels and use a rubber mallet to knock it down into place. A normal hammer will work too, if you put a piece of scrapwood under it.   **3 CLAMPING TIPS.** Put clamps near the top and bottom, keeping them clear of the protruding dowels but as close to them as possible. You'll need one at the middle, too. In this case, I used a wood block to keep the clamp pressure focused on the top, missing the ends of the dowels.   **4 ONE LAST TOUCH.** Before putting the table aside to dry for a few hours, take a minute to remove the glue squeeze-out in the inside corners while it's still soft. Use a chisel as a scraper, cleaning it off between swipes.

FIX MISTAKES WITH GAP-FILLING GOOP

Part of being a good builder is learning how to fix mistakes. These happen to the best of us.

1 OOPS. The drill blew out a few of the holes in this soft wood. **2 DIY WOOD PUTTY.** Save your sanding dust and mix it with yellow glue to make a batch of putty. Mix it thick with more dust than glue. **3 FILL AND WAIT.** Stuff the gaps with goop, use a stick of wood and your fingertip to smooth it out, and wait three or four hours for it to dry fully. **4 LEVEL WITH SANDPAPER.** Your sanding block strikes again. Work up through the grits as usual. **5 NOT PERFECT BUT NOT BAD.** The glue darkens the patch a little, but the fix blends in pretty well if you resist the urge to point it out to your friends!

LEVEL ALL THE JOINTS

The dowels, tenons, and wedges are all sticking out. Here's how to cut them off cleanly and level them with the surrounding wood for a beautiful result.

1 THE FRIDGE MAGNET TRICK. Put a large flat refrigerator magnet on the inside face of the saw. That will keep it off the surface so you can saw off the protruding joinery without damaging the wood below.

2 SANDING BLOCK FINISHES THE JOB. Use your sandpaper block with 80-grit paper to finish leveling the joints, and then work up through the grits to bring the surface back to 220-grit. A sharp block plane would be even better here, but I'm saving that for the next book!   **3 SAME THING ON THE TOP.** Flip the table over on its side to saw off the excess dowels, and use the sanding block to make them flush and smooth.   **4 ANOTHER SCRAPER.** This one is a paint scraper with a carbide blade, great for removing dried glue from flat surfaces.   **5 LEVEL ALL THE JOINTS.** Despite your best efforts, there will be some misalignment between the sides and top. Sand them flush, starting with 80-grit paper again. Go across the grain at first for faster wood removal, and then sand with the grain, working up through all the grits for a scratch-free surface.

TRANSFORMING TABLE WILL TRANSFORM YOUR SKILLS

SMOOTH FINISH

I recommend an oil finish here. Pine is soft and dents easily (which just adds to the charm of the piece) and the oil finish is easy to repair by simply wiping more on.

1 BREAK THE EDGES. Use your block with 150-grit paper to put a light bevel (chamfer) on all the edges. Soft edges feel better and look better, too, but don't overdo it. **2 SO PRETTY.** Grab some disposable vinyl gloves again, and pour on the oil in a small puddle where you can, spreading it with paper towels and wiping off the excess. Let the first coat dry, sand lightly by hand with 220-grit paper, and then put on one more coat.

11

celebrate with music

THE PREVIOUS PROJECT was real furniture and pretty intense, so let's end with some pure fun. This passive smartphone speaker is quick and easy to make, and its acoustic secret is just cool.

The science behind a passive speaker is simple. If you've ever stuck your phone in the bottom of a cup or glass to hear the music better, you know how it works: The sound bounces around the bottom, expanding and growing as it moves up and out. Store-bought versions are more sophisticated but work on the same principle.

As soon as someone discovered the cup trick, DIYers started making their own passive speakers, often from wood. These range from not so great looking to nice but not so easy to build, so I went searching for the sweet spot between. The solution was building in layers.

A SOUND SANDWICH

A passive speaker has three jobs: It needs to hold your device, direct its sound down a small channel, and send it into a big opening that broadcasts outward. So how to work with the tools in this book and create those three openings, with one of them being completely hidden?

ALL WOOD AMPLIFIER. This little block reminds me of an old-school transistor radio.

On one of my many trips to the local home center, I found small boards in various widths and thicknesses, designed for woodworking projects. The varied thicknesses let me visualize a sandwich, with a thicker back and front, and a thin layer in the middle that could both hold the phone and create the little sound tunnel. And the width of the boards, at 5½ in., was just right. With the right sequence of cutting and gluing, I would end up with all the nooks and crannies I needed, in one compact block.

The only downside to these small boards was the limited wood selection. I had to choose between red oak and poplar (I chose the latter). But if you have a friend with a thickness planer, you could use any wood you like for your three layers.

By the way, I used the round-hole jig from the cornhole game again, this time to cut the big speaker hole into the two front layers of the block.

After drawing up the design, the whole enterprise was still in doubt. I knew I could build my mazy block using only the tools in this book, but I still didn't know if the thing would work. For that I had to make a prototype. When it was done, I pressed the play button on my phone, stuck my phone in the block, held my breath, and listened.

If the little block hadn't amplified the sound—significantly—I'm not sure I would have known what to do to fix it. I never did get that advanced degree in acoustical engineering. But it did work—amazingly. My 12-year-old daughter likes her floating shelves just

SPOT THE DIFFERENCE? On this version I left the short outside corners square. Pick the model you like best, or do something totally different. Keep the acoustic parts similar though.

CELEBRATE WITH MUSIC

GIVE POPLAR A TAN. Use whatever wood you can find in ½-in. and ¾-in. thicknesses, at 5½ in. wide. I went with poplar, which starts out looking greenish, but turns creamy brown when you put the finished project in the sun.

fine, but this magic speaker actually impressed her (she stole it immediately). It only took me 11 chapters to do that.

building is fun, so dive in!

The final lesson of this book is that building stuff is supposed to be fun—especially if it's a hobby. Build whatever you want, however you want to build it. That's what the Maker movement is all about. People hack their phones, pillage junkyards and flea markets for found items, and mix digital design and 3D printing with old-school skills like woodworking, sewing, and soldering to turn their high-tech world into something human and handmade.

If traditional woodworking is what inspires you, that's fine too. Load up on Lie-Nielsen® and Lee Valley hand tools, learn to sharpen and use them, and Zen out in your quiet workspace.

The point is that you don't have to play by anyone else's rules. All my favorite makers approached their work with fearless integrity. Look up Wharton Esherick, the artist, sculptor, and woodworker in Pennsylvania.

He invented furniture no one had seen before, built walls from tinted concrete, and hand-made every non-square corner and funky curve of his amazing house in the woods. When he hit a termite nest in the cellar, he just kept digging, opening up the center of the house into a three-story "sculpture well," which he filled with weird tall woodcarvings.

You don't have to be Wharton Esherick. Be you. My deepest hope for this book is that it inspires you to dive in, to become a maker and builder of things, whatever that means to you.

As I write this last chapter, I'm replacing the old fence around our backyard with my own creation: corrugated steel roofing panels framed by wood posts and crosspieces. It's beautiful to us, so it's beautiful. Fence, lamp, bench, bottle opener, it doesn't matter. Build your world.

LAY OUT THE MIDDLE LAYER

All of the layers start out 18 in. long. The project gets chopped to final length only after the layers are glued together. Start by laying out the middle layer, which is the thinnest.

1 SPEAKER HOLE. After laying out the ends of the final block, find the center of the speaker hole, set your compass, and pencil in the big circle. **2 PHONE POCKET.** Draw a line 1 in. away from the edge and set the phone there, ensuring it is square to the block. Move it up until the volume controls are above the top edge and accessible. Then trace around the phone. After tracing, add ¹⁄₁₆ in. or so on each side so the phone will slide in easily. **3 NOW THE CHANNEL.** Mark the edges of the speaker, sliding the phone side to side in its pocket to make sure none of the speaker holes will be covered. Then draw the two different arcs that create the channel.

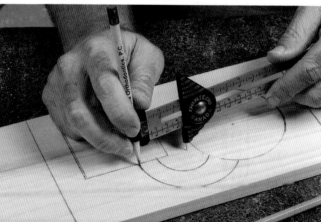

LAY OUT THE TOP LAYER

Use the middle layer to lay out the top one, which is a thicker ³⁄₄ in.

1 SAME SPEAKER HOLE. After laying out the end lines, make this speaker hole the same as the last one. **2 SMALLER POCKET.** Use the pocket in the middle layer to lay out this one, moving the lines in by ¼ in. on the sides. Use the square to finish the layout, remembering to leave the bottom of the pocket shorter too, and draw a roughly ¼-in. radius at each bottom corner.

CUT THE MIDDLE LAYER

This layer needs its pocket and channel cut out. Save the speaker hole for later.

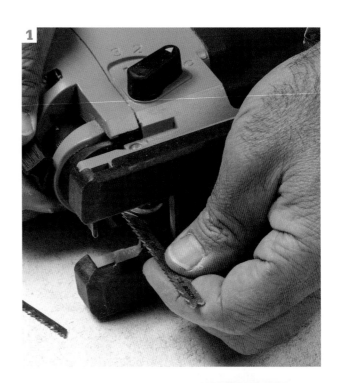

1 BEST BLADE. For the straight walls of this pocket, use a blade designed for making very smooth cuts in hardwoods. These blades are widely available and make an amazing difference. **2 CUT OUT THE POCKET.** Start with straight cuts down the sides. Then make a curving cut down to the bottom edge, which will allow you to make a straight cut across the bottom. Note how the extra board length leaves room for clamping. **3 BLADE CHANGE.** You'll need to use a narrower blade to form the tight curves of the channel. **4 CUT THE CHANNEL.** Make these cuts as smooth as possible, and finish by cutting into the speaker area, which will be removed later. **5 SAND IT SMOOTH.** Use 120-grit paper to remove the sawmarks in the channel, creating a smooth path for the sound. A piece of a rubber mat makes a good backer for smoother sanding.

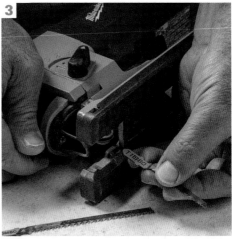
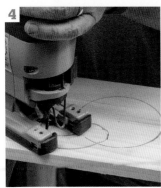

CUT THE POCKET IN THE TOP LAYER

This will also get a big speaker hole, but only after being glued to the middle layer.

1 FRONT POCKET. You'll need the narrower blade for the pocket in the front layer, which has rounded corners. Stay inside the layout lines for these curves. You'll finish them with sandpaper next. **2 SAND THE SIDES.** Start with 120-grit paper and work up to 150-grit. Sand the sides with your normal block. **3 SAND THE BOTTOM.** It helps to clamp the board on edge, using hand screws as we did with the lamp frame in Chapter 9. Use a ½-in. dowel to form smooth curves at the bottom edges, and then a narrow block to flatten the bottom edge.

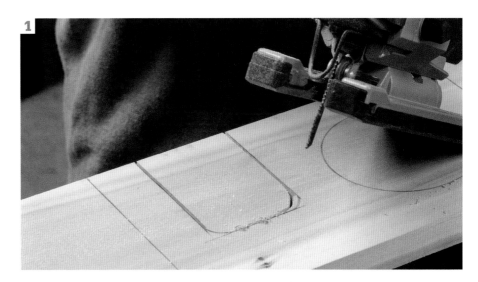

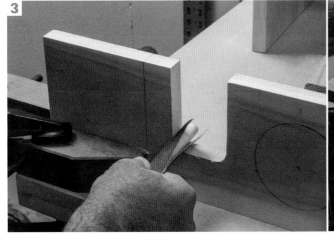

LAMINATE TWO LAYERS

Lamination is the technical word for gluing wide things together, like the top and middle layers of this project.

1 THE CLIPPED-BRAD TRICK. As I did earlier in the book, I'll be using little ½-in.-long brads to keep the layers from sliding out of alignment as they are glued and clamped. Drive in the brads, keeping them away from future sawcuts. Then clip off their heads, leaving a short, sharp point sticking up.   **2 CAREFUL GLUING.** Brush on plenty of glue, but keep it light near the edges of the pocket and channel so you don't get a lot of squeeze-out that needs to be fussed with after the fact.   **3 ALIGN THE PIECES.** Bring the top layer down on the middle one, using your fingertips to make sure they are aligned. Check the pencil lines for side-to-side alignment too.   **4 LOTS OF CLAMPS.** Use a couple of clamps to press the layers together, making sure they stay aligned. The tiny brads will let you make slight shifts. Then put clamps everywhere you can fit them to make sure there are no gaps between the layers. But don't bother clamping outside the end lines.

CUT THE SPEAKER HOLES

We'll use the same jigsaw gizmo we used to make the cornhole game, so check Chapter 3 for reference.

1 DRILL A STARTER HOLE. I used a ½-in. drill here to make a big hole for the jigsaw blade. You'll need to overlap the layout line at the edge slightly in order to get the blade into position to cut, but try to minimize that overlap, as it will show at the edge of the finished speaker hole. **2 SAME CIRCLE-CUTTING JIG.** As you did for the big holes in the cornhole boards, you need a small piece of thin plywood, a tight-fitting nail hole in both the plywood and the center of the circle, and a hole where the blade will drop in, in this case 1¾ in. from the nail hole. I drew some extra guidelines to help me here. Then I attached double-faced tape to the jigsaw base. **3 ROUND WE GO.** Line up the jigsaw on the little plywood piece, square to the edge, with the blade passing through it. Then hit the trigger and let the jigsaw work its way around the circle. If you notice the blade starting to flex left or right, the tape will let you steer the saw a little bit to correct its course. **4 SMOOTH HOLE.** Pull the saw away when you are done, remove the big wood plug from the center nail, and admire your work.

FINISH OFF THE BLOCK

The back layer is just a blank slab of ¾-in.-thick wood. Once it's on, you can chop the block to size.

1 BRADS AND GLUE. Use more clipped brads, and once again keep the glue away from the inside corners where squeeze-out will be hard to remove.   **2 ALIGN AND CLAMP.** Lay down the back layer, align it on the lower pieces, and then use lots of clamps to apply strong, even pressure. Once again, check that the layers remain aligned at the edges.   **3 CHOP AND SAND.** After waiting an hour or two, chop off the block at your layout lines, scrape away any glue squeeze-out, and rough-sand the edges flat. The speaker will work great right now (give it a spin!), but let's make it look even better.

SET UP YOUR ROUTER TABLE

We'll use the simple router-table setup from the previous chapter to make the speaker more sleek and stylish.

1 BIGGER BIT, BIGGER HOLE. The roundover bit is bigger than the small straight bit in the last chapter, so use a hole saw, spade bit, or Forstner bit to drill a big hole about 8 in. from the end of your MDF table panel. Clamp a scrap board underneath before drilling.   **2 RIGHTY-TIGHTY.** Load a 3/8-in.-dia. bearing-guided bit in the router's chuck. You might have to leave more of the bit sticking out of the chuck than normal in order to reach the top of the table.   **3 ATTACH THE ROUTER.** This time I just left the plastic base plate on the router, drilling through it where needed to allow me to drive screws into the router table.   **4 LEVEL THE BIT.** Adjust the height of the router so the bottom of the roundover bit is just level with the tabletop.

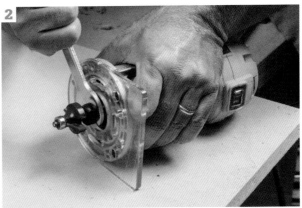

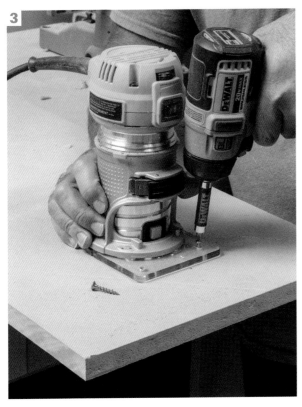

ROUTER TABLE MAKES SHORT WORK OF ROUNDOVERS

You could hold the router by hand to make all of these roundovers, but it would be tricky to balance the base on some parts of the workpiece. The table supports the block completely as you move it past the bit.

1 READY TO ROLL. This simple router table is nothing more than a piece of MDF clamped to your workstation. We'll start by rounding the edges of the speaker hole.   **2 START WITH THE BIG HOLE.** Drop the hole down over the spinning bit, without touching it, and then move the block until you feel the bearing riding the edge of the hole. Start moving the block right away, in a clockwise direction, against the rotation of the bit. Keep it moving steadily until you have gone around the circle a couple of times, and you should get a nice clean result.   **3 NOW THE PHONE POCKET.** Start on the right side of the pocket, as shown below. Press steadily against the bearing as you run the bit down one edge, along the bottom, and back out the other side. Keep the block moving steadily and you'll minimize the burn marks.   **4 DONE IN MINUTES.** After rounding the outside edges (front and back), the sleek look is complete.

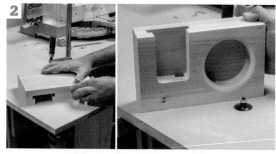

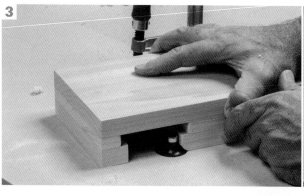

FINISHING TOUCHES

This project is small and the finish is just a few coats of oil, so you'll be done in no time. Once again the oil finish is Minwax Tung Oil, which is easy to apply and brings out the beauty of the wood.

1 A BIT OF SANDING. Use your sanding block to do the flat areas, working up from 120-grit to 220-grit. On the roundovers, a flexible backer is the ticket. The rubber backer works in the tight curves, too, getting rid of the last few burn marks and smoothing all the transitions from round to flat. **2 SIMPLE OIL FINISH.** Start in the openings, pouring in a small puddle of finish and spreading it into all the tight corners. Then do the flat surfaces, front and back. Wipe off the excess and let each coat dry for a few hours before sanding it lightly with 220-grit paper, folded and held in your hand. Then wipe off the dust and apply the next coat. Repeat until you are happy with the look.

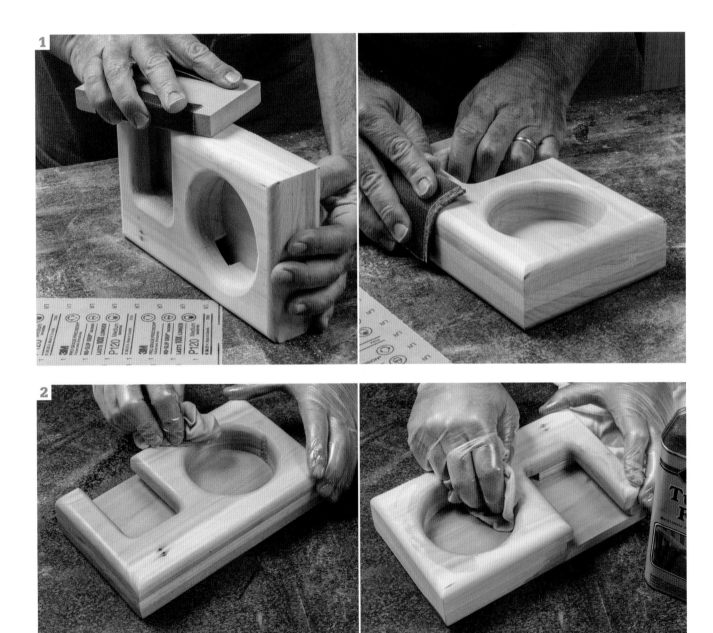

METRIC EQUIVALENTS

INCHES	CENTIMETERS	MILLIMETERS	INCHES	CENTIMETERS	MILLIMETERS
1/8	0.3	3	13	33.0	330
1/4	0.6	6	14	35.6	356
3/8	1.0	10	15	38.1	381
1/2	1.3	13	16	40.6	406
5/8	1.6	16	17	43.2	432
3/4	1.9	19	18	45.7	457
7/8	2.2	22	19	48.3	483
1	2.5	25	20	50.8	508
1 1/4	3.2	32	21	53.3	533
1 1/2	3.8	38	22	55.9	559
1 3/4	4.4	44	23	58.4	584
2	5.1	51	24	61	610
2 1/2	6.4	64	25	63.5	635
3	7.6	76	26	66.0	660
3 1/2	8.9	89	27	68.6	686
4	10.2	102	28	71.7	717
4 1/2	11.4	114	29	73.7	737
5	12.7	127	30	76.2	762
6	15.2	152	31	78.7	787
7	17.8	178	32	81.3	813
8	20.3	203	33	83.8	838
9	22.9	229	34	86.4	864
10	25.4	254	35	88.9	889
11	27.9	279	36	91.4	914
12	30.5	305			